E. A. Brayley (Edward Arthur Brayley) Hodgetts

In the Track of the Russian famine

The Personal Narrative of Journey through the Famine Districts of Russia

E. A. Brayley (Edward Arthur Brayley) Hodgetts

In the Track of the Russian famine
The Personal Narrative of Journey through the Famine Districts of Russia

ISBN/EAN: 9783744746915

Printed in Europe, USA, Canada, Australia, Japan

Cover: Foto ©Andreas Hilbeck / pixelio.de

More available books at **www.hansebooks.com**

In the Track

OF THE

Russian Famine

The Personal Narrative of a Journey through the Famine Districts of Russia

BY

E. A. BRAYLEY HODGETTS

London
T. FISHER UNWIN
PATERNOSTER SQUARE

1892

PREFACE.

―o―

THIS little book professes to be nothing more than a reprint of a series of letters on the Russian Famine, which appeared in the London and Provincial press during last winter as *Reuter's Special Service.*

I was told that they had attracted some attention, and that their republication as a book might be acceptable.

By the kind permission of Reuter's Telegram Company, and partly at their suggestion, I am now able to present these letters to the public in the form of a separate work. They were written under many disadvantages, and may leave much to be desired from the point of view of literary workmanship. One merit, however, they have; they give a truthful and unbiassed account of what I saw.

I cannot refrain from seizing this opportunity for publicly expressing my gratitude to those Russian and English friends, to whom I am so deeply indebted for advice and assistance during my journey.

To the Russian official authorities I also feel deeply grateful. I was never once interfered with or molested, and always experienced the greatest kindness and readiness to impart information and afford facilities.

Finally, I must not omit to register my thanks to Reuter's Telegram Company, to whose initiative and enterprise I owe one of the most interesting episodes in my life.

E. A. BRAYLEY HODGETTS.

Paris, *May* 1892.

CONTENTS.

CHAPTER I.

INTRODUCTION, ... 1

CHAPTER II.

TULA, ... 13

CHAPTER III.

THE WIDOW AND THE PRINCE, ... 22

CHAPTER IV.

THE PEASANTS OF RIASAN, ... 40

CHAPTER V.

COUNT TOLSTOI'S KITCHENS, ... 59

CHAPTER VI.

AN INTELLECTUAL CENTRE, ... 75

CHAPTER VII.

THE VILLAGES OF VORONESH, ... 87

CHAPTER VIII.
TAMBOFF, ... 107

CHAPTER IX.
THE GOLDEN PORT OF THE VOLGA, . . . 124

CHAPTER X.
SARATOFF ABORIGINES, ... 134

CHAPTER XI.
THE KOTZEBUE ESTATE, ... 147

CHAPTER XII.
THE STORY OF THE GERMAN COLONISTS, . . 159

CHAPTER XIII.
NIJNI-NOVGOROD, ... 178

CHAPTER XIV.
THE PEASANTS OF NIJNI, ... 190

CHAPTER XV.
A DRIVE TO KAZAN, ... 204

CHAPTER XVI.
THE TARTARS, ... 217

CHAPTER XVII.
CONCLUSION, ... 235

In the Track of the Russian Famine.

----o----

CHAPTER I.

INTRODUCTION.

I HAD had a particularly hard year as Reuter's agent in Berlin, and wanted a holiday badly. In reply to my application, I was asked whether I would not prefer to do the Russian famine. Now, I had lived twelve years in Russia, knew the language and the people well, and the offer was very tempting. It was pleasant to think that I should be able to revisit the scenes of my boyhood, look up the friends of my youth, and all at somebody else's expense. Time produces great changes. Friends whom I had left striplings had, as I knew, grown up into celebrities, others had accumulated the goods of this world, and had waxed rich and prosperous. Some had taken to themselves wives, and multitudinously increased the population; others had, alas, found this journey of life a hard road to travel, they had stumbled by the way-side, fallen and died. I must confess that to hear of my old friends, and to see the old places, these were the motives that animated me when I accepted my mission. As to the famine, well, that was a matter of very much minor importance. Perhaps there was a famine, perhaps not. I would try to ascertain, and do the best I could. If I got turned out of the country by the police, that would be a capital personal advertisement, and if I should by any chance be killed or eaten by the starving peasant, why, we can only die once, and once we all must die. It was, therefore, with a light heart and a peaceful mind that I boarded the sleeping-car of my train in Berlin. Shall I say that I regret having accepted the mission? Certainly not. But had I known how long it would take me, and what sights would meet me, what loneliness I should experience, I would certainly not have entered upon it in quite so light-hearted a spirit. On my return to London, the first question asked by the nice old maiden ladies of my acquaintance was, whether the accounts in the papers of the famine in Russia were not exaggerated? It took me some time to explain that, as I had myself written them, I was bound to vindicate their accuracy. I will, however, now quite frankly and honestly declare that there is really and truly no exaggeration in the picture I have painted. Indeed, I think the best evidence in favour of my truthfulness will be found in the fact that the blacking bottle of the censor did not make illegible any one of my articles. Russian officials of exalted rank assured me that all I had said was perfectly true, and nobody has accused me of animus or malice. I have described what I have seen, and have generally left the facts to speak for themselves.

When I arrived in Moscow, I was fortunate in finding Count Tolstoi there, and had a long chat with him. This eccentric genius seemed to place the whole blame of the present decline in the economic condition of the peasantry at the door of the railways. His first remedy was to encourage the manufacture of basket-shoes, and of village industries generally.

In Moscow, everybody was complaining of bad trade, manufacturers as well as merchants. When the peasant starves, industry and commerce are at a stand-still.

I did not remain long in Moscow, but proceeded at once almost to Tula, and then commenced my visits amongst the peasantry. The condition of these unhappy people is indeed deplorable, and what makes their case worse, is, that with most of them starvation is chronic. The hard, unpalatable truth is this: the Russian peasant is a charming, amiable, good-natured fellow, possessed of no vicious proclivities beyond a certain fondness for drink—very excusable in a cold climate—and absolutely without a single disagreeable virtue. He is lazy, thriftless, untruthful, and thoroughly picturesque and charming. That he is no better than he is is hardly his fault, as I have abundantly shown, but his generally necessitous condition places him now at a very great disadvantage—nobody can tell whether he is starving more acutely than usual. A careful inspection of the distressed districts has convinced me that the present state of the peasant is indeed as bad as it can be. But whether it is possible to confer any permanent benefits upon him, that is a much more difficult question. Personally, I have little sympathy for, and less faith in the political agitators of Russia. They are all faddists more or less and have very few sound and practical ideas. Besides, they are only playing at revolution, and have absolutely no chance at present of success. I had an interview with one of these leaders in Moscow, and his utterances, though deserving of reproduction, show what little practical common sense these people have.

This is what he said :—" The present famine is not a bolt from the blue—a single phenomenon that has come suddenly, and will as suddenly depart. It is the natural consequence of thirty years' bad management, and will become chronic. If it had not occurred this year it would have occurred some other year. It is an inevitable result of a series of causes. The peasants may be relieved, we may buy corn for them and feed them, but how are we to give them back their horses and cattle? They have already killed half of them. This is one consideration. There is yet another. These sixteen or seventeen provinces which are now suffering from want are not the only ones which will be in need of help next spring. Fifty, not sixteen, provinces will be in a state of starvation. Then, those governments which have had good harvests are not the self-supporting ones. They have generally to import corn in the winter and early spring for themselves. This year their state is much worse, seeing they have exported all the corn they could spare to the famine-stricken districts. What their condition will be in the spring you may imagine. The state of the peasantry is extremely unsatisfactory. They are at once apathetic and desperate. They are prostrate in the face of the terrible calamity that has befallen them; but their apathy cannot last. Risings may be expected. The peasants believe it to be the Tzar's duty to feed them. I have heard them talk as follows:—'The Tzar must feed us, and if he does not, we must choose another.' What is society to do in the face of such a feeling? How are we to prevent a cataclysm. The little influence and energy which our society possesses, the government endeavours to take from it. There are only two forces which keep the State together—the Church and the army; and the present regime has made for itself enemies in both—not small, insignificant enemies, but powerful and influential ones. I will not mention names for fear of drawing attention to them, but I think it is very improbable that the soldiers, if called from the Polish frontier to shoot down their starving fathers and brothers, would be likely to obey their orders; but if the Polish frontier should be denuded of troops, and the country generally disturbed, I cannot conceive that Austria and Germany would look on quietly and not make an effort to render harmless for a time the power which they have learned to regard as their greatest and most dangerous foe. We have made enemies not only amongst our neighbours, but in our own house. The inhabitants of the Baltic provinces, once our most loyal subjects, are now our enemies. We have now not only a German question there, we are creating an Esthonian, a Lithuanian, and any number of questions. Finland we have also stirred up against us; but not content with these achievements, we are now elaborating a Tartar and an Armenian question. Of Poland I need not speak. You have heard how the peasantry regard the Tzar. They have no notion of legitimacy. One Tzar is as good as another. They obey the institution; they do not understand the legitimacy of the succession. As it happens, the present government has had the misfortune to make an enemy who may become very useful in the hands of agitators. I mean the young grand Grand Duke Michael Michaelovitch. He is very popular. We are living in terrible times. Our society is sunk in materialism, and cares for nothing but self-enjoyment, and the peasant has ceased to be the thoughtless Tzar-worshipper of the past. Besides, there appears to be a party at the head of affairs which is composed of Nihilists in disguise. They are Nihilists, only they have altered their methods, and they are leading the country to ruin and disaster in the most loyal fashion in the world. I regard this famine as a blessing in disguise. It may rouse us and show us the pitfalls to which we are going."

Interesting and even true all this is, but it is wild and much too sanguine. Russia is not ripe for revolution, and never will be. The peasant is much too cute, and has too much natural common sense to suffer himself to be led away by agitators. Besides, how is revolution to be made? A regiment of Cossacks would almost suffice to keep the whole of Russia quiet. The population is too sparse, communications are too imperfect, and there are no really important centres of population.

My own belief is, that what is wanted is education, more than anything else. The peasant wants moral as well as intellectual teaching. He is still little better than an amiable savage, and generations must pass before he will make any appreciable progress. In the meantime, a little freedom of the press, and some liberty of discussion, might do no harm. More important for Russia, as a civilised power, is it to try to make of her peasant an economic unit, instead of the helpless atom he is. Some kind of independence he must get, and that soon, and this the governing classes in Russia will have to recognise before long. As for the abuses that obtain, they are inseparable from the circumstances of the case. Without a press, without a single safe-guard, Russia has been the prey of self-seekers from time immemorial. What is most to be regretted is, that the officials are often more honest than the private individuals. Public-spirited unselfishness is very rare, and is not understood. I remember a gentleman, cultivated and refined, saying in the presence of a large company of people, who were all discussing the famine and the means of relieving it, that he did not believe any respectable person ever did anything for nothing, and that he was quite sure that the people who were helping the starving poor had mostly some selfish ends, and I am not sure that he was not right.

CHAPTER II.

TULA.

TULA is just six hours by rail due south from Moscow. It is the capital of one of the most prosperous provinces in the Tzar's dominions. There is no actual famine here. Why, then, have I broken my journey at this place? Well, I had two reasons. It is here and in the adjoining province of Riazan that the old Russian aristocracy and the true Russian life are to be found, and I had been fortunate enough to secure introductions to influential personages in those two provinces which ought to prove most serviceable to me. But I had a still stronger reason, in the fact that the Zemstvo of the Government of Tula was then sitting, and it is not every day an English journalist has an opportunity of listening to the debates of a Russian provincial administrative body.

Tula is popularly supposed to be the Russian Birmingham. To the superficial observer it is merely a village, and not a particularly fine one. In Moscow the traveller is already impressed with the fact that he is in a country where the population is not yet inconveniently dense, where space is no object, and where land has little value. Everything is on a larger scale than in overcrowded central Europe. The air is clearer, the houses stand comfortably in large courts and gardens, and everybody has plenty of breathing space. This impression is strengthened when the traveller arrives at Tula. There are plenty of houses of only one storey in the principal street. There are several, however, with a first floor, the hotels, for instance; and a few Government buildings have a second floor. The width of the streets is out of all proportion to the height of the buildings, and the latter look quite lost in the vast space which separates them.

Yet Tula is a manufacturing town of some importance. There is a Government small arms factory, a cartridge factory, and several metal works. Brass ware, notably samovars, and all manner of metal industries, are well represented. The factories do not intrude themselves unpleasantly upon the eye. The shops in the principal streets hardly rise to the level of those of an English village, but the chemists have magnificent premises. Like Moscow, Tula has a bazaar, and, like Moscow, it has a Kremlin, the ancient fortification of the town. But, unlike Moscow, the Kremlin of Tula has no magnificent buildings. It has only two churches.

The genesis of these Kremlins is interesting; the word is supposed to de derived from the Russian equivalent for flint, because the old walls which were erected as a protection against the Tartars were constructed of this material. The nobles and knyazes used to have their palaces inside these walls, and the merchants and traders used to erect their booths outside them, and do business with the strangers who travelled across the land. In times of war the merchants would forsake their booths, and take refuge behind the walls. Thus these booths have become the recognised feature of every Russian town. They are called the " Gostinny Dvor," or the Strangers' Court, for here also the travellers used to put up.

The province of Tula is a little kingdom in the very heart of the most industrial part of Russia. I therefore expected to see considerable stir, in view of the fact that the Zemstvo was in session. The Zemstvo is a much more important institution than we are accustomed to believe. It is the county council, the local government board, of the province, and has considerable powers. The meetings of the Zemstvo of a province always take place in the House of Nobles. The magnificent hall of this assembly, in Tula, is ornamented with portraits of the present Emperor, the late Emperor, and the Empress Catherine. The handsome marble bust of

Alexander II., with the inscription, "To the liberator of the peasants," has been placed in this hall, which is in white and gold. Along each side of the hall stand magnificent white columns with gilt capitals. The chairs provided for the nobles are white, with the occupant's crown painted upon the back. An air of magnificence and grandeur prevades the place. In this gorgeous council chamber, seated round a long table which, like the houses in the streets of Tula, seemed lost in this vast expanse of splendour, were about twenty-five more or less elderly gentlemen, all having that noble and distinguished bearing which characterises the Russian aristocrat. They were mostly princes. They were presided over by a most imposing personage in a blue dress coat with gold buttons. He wore his orders and decorations. His manner was courteous and grave. Politeness but faintly describes the prevalent tone. Handsome and portly, the mouth of an orator, the voice of a child, the president looked like a veritable *fin de*

B

siècle Jupiter in uniform, capable of apologising to the world for having so inconsiderately created it.

The meeting was open to the public, but like the army on the stage of a transpontine theatre, the public was represented by two individuals, myself and a lame gentleman. It was impossible not to feel lonely in that great hall, with its white columns and gold mouldings. In a wilderness of splendour, lost and neglected, distrusted by the Government which had instituted it, neglected by the people for whose benefit it was constituted, sat and deliberated the Zemstvo of the Province of Tula, the first rudimentary form of Russian self-government. The meeting was to commence at twelve, but owing to the difficulty of making a quorum, it did not actually begin before one.

The principal subject of discussion was naturally the famine. It was easy to discover that there was a party of retrenchment and reform, and another of benevolence. The benevolents carried the day. A stout and venerable gentleman, with a red face, a bald head, and a general appearance of having walked out of one of Dickens's novels, triumphantly pleaded the cause of the famine-stricken people. The question was not very revolutionary or alarming. It was simply to petition Government for the loan of three hundred thousand roubles, or for power to raise such a loan, in view of the prevalent distress in certain districts—the loan to be obtained without interest if possible, and in any case to bear not more than four per cent. The Opposition objected to the presentation of this petition, upon the ground that the small district councils had already petitioned the Government, and that it would be derogatory to the dignity of the Provincial Council to support these petitions, seeing that the district councils had thought proper to ignore it. But the benevolent gentleman would not hear of such a policy. He maintained that it was the duty of the Zemstvo to come to the aid of the distressed. Somebody had said that the Zemstvo was not a benevolent institution, and this seemed to enrage the champion of the peasantry extremely. He vented his wrath upon the member who had used such arguments, and his wrath was terrible to see. He shook his head, his voice quaked and rose high and shrill to the lofty ceiling of the gorgeously decorated hall, and his views prevailed. He pointed out that the real question to discuss, instead of raising objections to the petition, was what measures the Zemstvo should take in the event of the Government rejecting it, and how they should set to work to find the requisite funds. This question was not entered into, however. The courteous chairman did not seem to think the moment opportune.

I was considerably surprised to find so little interest taken in this meeting of the Zemstvo, and the discussion of these important questions. For Tula is not in a prosperous condition, and the effects of the famine are felt here more acutely than in Moscow. Many hands are out of employment, and the factories are doing bad business. The Zemstvo seemed to be conscious of its own impotence. The whole proceedings impressed one with a sense of the extreme difficulty of governing a country like Russia from one central authority; while side by side with this feeling was the conviction that the people are far too backward and far too apathetic to govern themselves.

CHAPTER III.

THE WIDOW AND THE PRINCE.

Travelling in Central Russia in mid-winter is never particularly pleasant, but when one's mission is to seek out and traverse the most famine-stricken districts, and investigate the condition of the suffering peasantry, it becomes almost a hardship. During my journey I have had to sleep in railway stations, in the squalid inns of towns which are little better than villages, and on the sofas of country gentlemen, upon whose hospitality I had thrown myself. My food consisted almost exclusively of bread made from rye and potato flour, and now and then a piece of frozen meat, washed down with the raw spirit called vodka, which, being interpretated, means "little water."

From Tula I travelled by train to Skopin, and there hired a troika, in which my journey from that point onwards has been accomplished. I had to spend a night at the interesting town of Skopin, and had been recommended to stop at a famous hotel kept by Konyakoff. It was a miserable collection of attics, which boasted neither carpets nor rugs. The floor emitted a curious pungent perfume. The waiter and boots and general attendant assured me that the bed was immune from entomological specimens. "How about fleas?" I asked. "Well, sir, there might be a flea or two. You can't prevent that, but perhaps you would like to have clean sheets." "What!" I shouted, "Have others been sleeping between these sheets?" "Only a few, sir." Regardless of expense I instantly ordered clean sheets, and spent a fairly good night, having passed the previous one on the unyielding bench of a railway station waiting-room. The traveller, who has been so far as St Petersburg and Moscow, will have pleasant recollections of a Russian troika, its handsome carpet and velvet cushions, the gaily-caparisoned horses, the mad pace through fields of snow, across the Neva to the islands, or along the high road from Moscow to Tver, to hear the gipsies sing at the gorgeous "Strelna." Very different, indeed, was my troika. Imagine an enormous packing-case on a sledge, one side left high for the back, the other cut down so as to enable the occupants to see out in front, with a little bench introduced for the driver—no seat for you but a quantity of straw, and on that straw a sack and some coarse Russian canvas—and you have the vehicle in which I have been careering across the snow-covered country. My back and my legs were at right angles. In this attitude, with the thermometer 15 degrees Réamur, and a wind sharp enough to shave you, I have sat motionless for five hours at a stretch, not knowing where I was going, and hardly caring, the vehicle jolting and bumping till every bone in my body ached again, while the villainous little horses kicked the snow in my face, and tinkled their monotonous bells. Far and wide not an object met the eye. Nothing could be seen, hour after hour, but a seemingly boundless expanse of snow. Occasionally the driver lost his way. How he found it again heaven only knows.

The horses fairly astonished me when I first saw them. They forcibly reminded me of those pantomime donkeys which are composed of two men and a skin; but the manner in which they did their work was a revelation. So far as I know, during the four days' hard driving, they did not get any food whatsoever, and as to breathing them, that was never even thought of. Their harness was an artistic arrangement of ropes. The centre horse had the inevitable "duga," a bow from which hung two abominable bells. The side horses, or gallopers, also carried bells, not quite so aggressive, but more dismal.

The driver was a lusty youth of about twenty,

with keen, laughing blue eyes, healthy canine teeth, and an expression of countenance which inspired respect. He was a perfectly healthy animal, fearing neither man nor devil, possessing no nerves whatever, and living on next to nothing, like his horses. He told me a good deal in the course of the journey about the state of the country. Some of the peasants, he said, don't taste food for three days together. When they get any they give it to their children.

What struck me most during my journey through the Government of Riasan was the almost total absence of trees. The enormous oak forests for which this province was once celebrated have all disappeared. This has naturally changed the climate, and the once fertile black earth of Central Russia is rapidly becoming an inhospitable desert. I am told by a landowner, from the Province of Orel, that there the same process is going on, and that the famous pine forests in which Turguenieff again, while the villainous little horses kicked the snow in my face, and tinkled their monotonous bells. Far and wide not an object met the eye. Nothing could be seen, hour after hour, but a seemingly boundless expanse of snow. Occasionally the driver lost his way. How he found it again heaven only knows.

The horses fairly astonished me when I first saw them. They forcibly reminded me of those pantomime donkeys which are composed of two men and a skin; but the manner in which they did their work was a revelation. So far as I know, during the four days' hard driving, they did not get any food whatsoever, and as to breathing them, that was never even thought of. Their harness was an artistic arrangement of ropes. The centre horse had the inevitable "duga," a bow from which hung two abominable bells. The side horses, or gallopers, also carried bells, not quite so aggressive, but more dismal.

The driver was a lusty youth of about twenty,

with keen, laughing blue eyes, healthy canine teeth, and an expression of countenance which inspired respect. He was a perfectly healthy animal, fearing neither man nor devil, possessing no nerves whatever, and living on next to nothing, like his horses. He told me a good deal in the course of the journey about the state of the country. Some of the peasants, he said, don't taste food for three days together. When they get any they give it to their children.

What struck me most during my journey through the Government of Riasan was the almost total absence of trees. The enormous oak forests for which this province was once celebrated have all disappeared. This has naturally changed the climate, and the once fertile black earth of Central Russia is rapidly becoming an inhospitable desert. I am told by a landowner, from the Province of Orel, that there the same process is going on, and that the famous pine forests in which Turguenieff was wont to shoot woodcock, and of which he has left us such charming descriptions, have vanished under the woodcutter's axe.

To hark back and sum up my observations in the Province of Tula, before entering upon a full description of Riasan, I may say, generally, that Tula has had an excellent wheat harvest, and as it is not a self-supporting province, but imports a great part of its bread, it cannot be said to have suffered very severely. In certain districts, indeed, the peasants are in a very desperate condition, but fortunately here the law of compensation comes in. The province is happy in the possession of several wealthy, intelligent, and public-spirited landowners, like M. Raphael Pissareff, for instance, the friend of Count Leon Tolstoi, a man of great wealth and culture, and a member of the Red-Cross Society. This gentleman has, by his means and example, done much to alleviate the lot of the peasants in his district. The same may be said of Professor Stebut, the eminent agriculturist, and many others. As these gentlemen are members of the Zemstvo of Tula, that body came early to the help of the necessitous peasants, and has been most energetic in dispensing belief.

Notwithstanding these more or less favourable circumstances, the feeling among the country gentlemen of Tula is most pessimistic. They are going to find work for their peasants, they are going to establish public ordinaries, they are already largely buying waggons of rye from the Caucasus, and they hope to tide over the distress till spring. But there is a general feeling that the famine may repeat itself next year, and a consensus of opinion that should this fear be realised, the Russian people will find themselves face to face with national bankruptcy.

In the province of Riasan, however, things are more desperate. The peasants are in a state of chronic semi-starvation, and hence there is but little margin for bad years. The last harvest was, however, nothing more than a figure of speech in some districts of the province, and hence the condition of the people is sad indeed.

My first visit on reaching this province was to the estate of a widowed lady, to whom I had a letter of introduction. A magnificent avenue of trees led to the house, and I expected to find at the end of it a stately mansion, instead of that, the residence of the proprietrix turned out to be a humble wooden cottage, less imposing, and certainly far less comfortable, than a porter's lodge in England. It had only one storey, and was as destitute of interior decorations as a barn, my hostess receiving me in a bare, white-washed room, with a low ceiling. The furniture consisted of an ancient piano, a horse-hair sofa, and a small table. There was not a single picture upon the walls. In striking contrast with these miserable surroundings was the tall, stately figure of the owner. Her hair was white, and her face full of beauty and tenderness. Her dress was homely, even shabby, but her bearing was instinct with nobility and grace. She had read the letter of introduction I had brought, and came forward to welcome me. In a few minutes tea was served, and about an hour later a dinner, which my hostess had evidently cooked herself. A young lady, who had come to open free dinners for the poor, a disciple of Count Tolstoi's, was staying with her, and while my hostess left the room, and prepared the dinner, we discussed the condition of the peasants at some length.

My hostess was of opinion that the peasants in her district were in the most hopeless condition. The Zemstvos, or local government councils, did indeed give the more distressed grain—about 36 lbs. per head—but this was intended principally for the children, and it was not sufficient to last a month. Then there were all kinds of hardships connected with this distribution. Lists had been made of the peasants requiring assistance; these lists were kept in each district, and based upon other lists which were supposed to give an inventory of the quantity of food and the size of each family. These inventories of food represented the stores of the peasant for the entire year, and terrible tales they told. Here was a man with six children, and only five poods, or 180 lbs. of grain, to last him through the winter. Others were absolutely destitute. Most of them had sold their cattle, many even their horses. Notwithstanding the trouble and care that had been taken in compiling these lists, they afforded no real index to the condition of the peasants, and the most frightful abuses occurred. Peasants comparatively well off were receiving aid, whilst others, who were literally starving, were classed as well-to-do. The saddest feature was, that the wealthy landlords were keeping away from their estates at present, and that the entire burden of looking after the shiftless peasants fell upon the poorer gentry, who were not much better off themselves.

"We do not like to speak about our own troubles," said this noble woman, "although things are so bad with us that you would scarcely believe me if I told you all. But in the face of the destitution of the peasants, we are ashamed to think of ourselves. We do what we can for them, but it is so little, so pitiable, that we are ashamed even of that."

"Where," I asked, "does the grain come from which the Zemstvos distribute?"

"Oh, that is brought from the nearest railway station by the peasants themselves, but it often arrives late. The peasants are now waiting for their monthly distribution, but they are always put off from day to day, and it does not come. Our peasants are marvels of endurance."

Many things did this good lady tell me of

her difficulties: how little she felt herself able to cope with the distress in her own neighbourhood, how inadequate and even visionary was the aid of the Zemstvo, how far away the Red Cross seemed to be.

"Some local Red-Cross Societies," she said, "are excellent — M. Pissareff's branch, for instance. The majority, however, have no funds, and before they can get money from St Petersburg a terrible time elapses. You see, we have little ourselves, and the wealthy merchants and manufacturers do not believe in the famine, and won't send any money."

I discovered subsequently that this version was not quite accurate. The fact is, that wealthy merchants have little faith in the Red-Cross Society. They wish to distribute themselves the money they are prepared to devote to the aid of the peasants. This the Government will not permit. The idea prevails among the public—and it is not altogether unwarranted—that a great deal of the money which is given to the Red-Cross Society never finds its way to the people.

"What will happen in the spring," my hostess remarked, "it is impossible to say. Probably the people, driven to desperation, will burn and pillage the neighbourhood. The worst of all is that there is no work."

When we had finished dinner, I rose to go.

"I am very sorry that I must let you go," she said, "but my little house is full."

Not knowing where I was to find a shelter for the night, I jumped into my sledge again, and set off for the estate of the Zemski Natchalnik, to whom also I had a letter. He was a prince, the scion of an illustrious house, and had been a sailor. I had hopes of getting a shakedown under his roof, though I had been warned that he was rough and uncultured, and had no sympathy with the peasants or their distress. After a long drive, we arrived towards nightfall at the prince's mansion. It was no bigger than a modern cottage of gentility, but it was, nevertheless, a very comfortable-looking dwelling. Was the prince at home? No, he was not; but would not the "barin" come in and warm himself. I entered, and sent my letter of introduction to the princess. She received me with great courtesy, and insisted on my staying till her husband came home, explaining that he was expected back that night or the following morning. To my great relief, my night's lodging was secured, and in a decent place. The prince had been to Japan, and his study was full of interesting objects, and had a very English appearance.

The princess, who had nothing to do during the long winter days and evenings, had spent her spare time in teaching herself foreign languages, by the aid of Ollendorf and dictionaries. I understood her better, however, when she spoke Russian, than when she imagined she was speaking English. We chatted pleasantly, and all she told me confirmed the impression I had already received, that the famine was a vague, intangible thing; that the peasants were, indeed, suffering terrible privations, but that there was no general starvation. In many cases, villages lying close to each other had had the most varying experience. One had had an excellent crop, while the other had had no crops at all. It was all a question of rain, and the rain had been very partial. The prince's own kitchen, I subsequently learned, was on the shortest of short commons, and my coachman had to go into the village to get supper—which consisted of black bread and salt—and feed his horses. When the prince arrived, which he did very soon, I found him to be a hale and hearty young sailor, full of energy, practical and smart, with very few dreamy theories, but a good deal of common-sense. He was the very man for the post he occupied. The Zemski Natchalniki are, to a certain extent, the guardians of the peasants. They have districts, sometimes forty versts wide, to inspect;

they hold rough courts, and inquire into cases; they preside over the peasant tribunals; have power to commute punishments, and to put peasants under arrest; but they have not, as is erroneously supposed, the right to administer corporal punishment.

While we were chatting, the starost, or mayor, of a neighbouring village, came to see the prince about a certain peasant, who owed a neighbour a sum of money, and had given him a bill of sale on all his goods and chattels. He had failed to meet his obligation, and his creditor wished to execute the bill of sale.

"What are we to do?" said the starost. "We cannot sell up and ruin the poor fellow."

"Send me the bill of sale, and I will stay execution for a year," said the prince.

I had a long conversation with him about his office. He told me the peasants looked up to him, appealed to him in all their disputes, came to him for advice, and entrusted their money to his keeping.

"Once," he said, "a fellow tried to bribe me. He shoved a lot of ten rouble notes into my hand."

"What did you do?"

The prince laughed, and looked shame-faced. "What was I to do? I thrashed him. I have never had bribes offered me since."

"Yours must be an interesting office," I said.

"Yes, but very trying. I spend my days driving about. My salary goes in office expenses. The Government are too fond of scribbling. They kill us with reports and correspondence, and now that we have been made presidents of the local Red-Cross Societies, we shall be simply buried in papers. By-the-bye, would you like to come to the inaugural meeting of our Red-Cross Society tomorrow?"

I need scarcely say that I accepted this proposal with alacrity. That night I was quartered in the study, and slept among a curious collection of Japanese armour, naval swords, loaded revolvers, Persian and Turcoman carpets. The library included an interesting collection of French classics of the eighteenth century.

CHAPTER IV.

THE PEASANTS OF RIASAN.

NEXT day, a two hours' drive in the face of a terribly cutting wind brought us to the residence of the landowner at whose estate the local branch of the Red-Cross Society was to be opened. This house, like most of the country houses in this district, would have been considered unfit for habitation by an English farmer. Many an English agricultural labourer lives in greater comfort than the majority of the Russian noblemen. The particular nobleman we came to see was young, handsome, and intelligent, and had a most charming and beautiful wife. The members of the proposed local branch of the Red-Cross

Society had assembled when we arrived. They consisted of two sleek, young, and extremely stupid-looking priests. There was a Jew, who looked out of his element; a German estate agent, energetic and practical; and a Circassian cossack in uniform, with fierce black eyes, and full of Oriental dignity. He, likewise, was an estate agent. An old lady was also present. The only country gentlemen in attendance were the prince and his host. After going through the formality of reading the bye-laws of the Red-Cross Society, the meeting resolved to constitute themselves a branch thereof.

Then came the question of funds. There was no money. The Circassian had given 100 roubles, a lady had sent 1000, and with this inadequate sum of £110, the Red-Cross Society, for a district having a population of 83,000 more or less starving peasants, was opened. Millions and millions have fallen into the coffers of the central committees of the Society at St Petersburg and Moscow, but where they go nobody knows. This want of funds is the *crux* of the present crisis. The gentry are little better off than the peasants; yet the latter, who are not tenants or feudal dependents, but proprietors of their own land, look upon all the aid they receive from the gentry as their due.

After a luncheon of boiled beef, black bread and vodka, to which the assembled company were all invited, I was taken round the villages in the neighbourhood, and inspected nearly every peasant's hut. Some of the sights that met my eye were so terrible and so disgusting that a feeling of nausea comes over me as I think of them now.

My mentor was the gentleman at whose house the meeting was held. He was wiry and energetic; but his regard for the peasants was more like that of a farmer for his cattle than a fellow-feeling. His views were not uninteresting, and they are those of his class. He considered that the peasants should be kept in subjection and made to work, and that the greatest mistake ever committed was to free them.

After a brisk drive in a sledge over the snow-clad plain, we arrived at the first village in our round of inspection, attended by the Elders of the place. We went into the first miserable hut of the wretched little row that constituted the village street. My friend entered unceremoniously and roughly, without knocking or calling. A kind of vapour poured out at the opened door. I bent my head and shoulders to avoid banging myself against the lintel, and we passed inside.

As soon as I could discern objects through the dense atmosphere that pervaded the cabin, I became aware of the presence of several human beings, whose appearance and attitude filled me with horror. In the background stood a wrinkled hag, a handkerchief tied round her head. The rest of her costume— consisting of a shirt, petticoat, and leggings —was squalid and wretched to the last degree.

To the right was an immense stove, and over this a broad shelf, on which several frightened children were huddled together. They looked dirty, unkempt, and savage beyond description. There was no floor. We were standing upon the bare ground. The hut was about twenty feet square by ten feet high. To the left was a plain deal table, over which hung the image of some patron saint. Under the latter, and at right angles, ran two benches. There was a third bench in front of the table, and a sort of settle at the end. This table and these benches, the only furniture the hut could boast of, had grown black with age and dirt. They were so filthy that I involuntarily gathered up the skirts of my fur coat, for fear of touching them. Running from the door to the stove was a beam or rafter, and on this were a few wretched dishes and cooking utensils. A fearful stench pervaded the hut.

Cap in hand, with trembling knees, haggard cheeks, and hollow eyes, stood the owner of this squalid dwelling, who bade us welcome with a cringing humility and a look of mingled cunning and fear, that reminded one of the wild beasts in a cage when the tamer has jumped in. Besides the old peasant and his wife, there were two young men and their wives; the parents, I realised, of the third generation cramped on that shelf over the stove. Talk of overcrowding in the London slums! I have seen something of that, but this beats anything that London could show. My guide looked round restlessly and insolently, his cap on his head, while the peasants stood uncovered.

"What bread have you got?" he said. "Show us your bread."

"We have no bread. We have had nothing to eat for three days, by God," they all sang in a sort of chorus.

"Nonsense, you have some bread,"

"Not a morsel; so help us, God."

They looked as though they had not eaten anything for weeks—not days.

We left their wretched hovel and entered their store-room opposite the entrance, and occupying the outer side of the hut. Here were a few empty boxes, nothing else. We went next to the barn and cattle-sheds. The barn was empty and bare. The roof had been taken down for fuel. Some of the neighbours had nothing but the skeletons of their barns left, and several had begun to consume the roofs of their huts. The cattle-sheds were also empty. The live stock of the family had been reduced to a single famished-looking sheep and a horse which was only a bag of bones. My friend turned round as though he were reading a lecture at the Polytechnic, and these accessories were objects of scientific demonstration, without life or feeling.

"You see," he said, this peasant is one of the poorest. He has no corn, no cattle, no food, yet he is not marked down for the receipt of relief until three weeks hence, because he is still able to work; and now we will go to the next."

I will spare the reader a dreary repetition of these heart-rending experiences. The same melancholy picture presented itself again and again. There were variations and incidents, however. Several peasants who protested that they had no bread were found to have entire loaves—and a Russian loaf is no trifle—of half-meal bread; that is, not coarse black bread, but rye bread mixed with wheat.

"Ah! you devils! You are living much too comfortably for me. Take their names out of the list for relief," said my mentor to the village Elder.

"Oh, master, little one, little father, nourisher of the people, don't be hard on us. It is Sunday."

"Very well, it shall be Sunday every day of the week with you."

In another hut we found the only occupants —a little girl of fourteen, with eyes red from crying, and two little children. "Where are your father and mother?" he asked. "They have gone," the child replied, "gone to the town to find work, and have not come back for a fortnight. I don't know what has happened to them, and I am left all alone with the children. I don't know what is going to become of me," and she recommenced crying, while the little children joined in the dismal wail.

The peasants seemed all to be perfectly used to summary inspection, and had indeed gone through this form time and again. They all made things appear worse than they were. It was, of course, absurd to suppose that an entire village had been without food for three days running, and indeed we frequently came by accident upon bread and flour sufficient for a day or two, and even for weeks. There can be little doubt that the average peasant weakens his case by overstating it. Many of the peasants live on from year to year in a chronic state of distress, and are accustomed to extort aid from the charitable. These have managed better this year than those who have hitherto been self-supporting. The latter do not know how to make their case appear sufficiently pitiable, and, in the general distress, are not considered deserving of exceptional aid. Most of the peasants hide any stores of bread, flour, and corn they may be lucky enough to possess. But the burning of their own roofs is a sign which leaves no room for doubt as to the acuteness of the distress.

Some of the food of these poor peasants was terrible to see. Broken bits of bread, collected through begging; some mildewed, others foul with dirt, lay together in the peasants' bread-baskets. Many of these peasants had pigs in their huts; some looked drunken and dissipated; a few haggard, with ominous black rings under the eyes, indicating hunger; but only a very few. All, however, looked like frightened animals, and huddled themselves together when we entered. The children hid themselves on the plank over the stove, and peeped at us when they thought we were not looking. The peasants seemed to have no furniture, no utensils, no property of any kind beyond their sheep-skins, their shirts, their wooden benches, wooden bowls, and wooden ladles. Signs of intellectual life there were none.

What struck me most during visits to these huts was, first of all, the appalling fact, which one scarcely realises until one is brought face to face with it, that the major part of the vast empire known as European Russia — namely, fifteen provinces — is in receipt of what we should call out-door relief. Imagine an entire country, about ten times the size of England, completely pauperised, the country gentry turned into guardians of the poor, the government a gigantic workhouse. That is the present state of Russia. There is, I still think, comparatively little actual starvation, but there is a complete standstill of all industrial and productive work, for the bad harvest has made itself felt in the towns, and the peasants, who come up to get work in factories, etc., come back disheartened or become itinerant beggars. The entire population seems to be on the tramp.

The next fact which strikes one forcibly is the absolute helplessness and self-abasement of the peasants. Notwithstanding the thirty years of self-government, more or less, which they have enjoyed in their Mirs, or village communes, the peasants seem to be as helpless and shiftless as they were while the serfs of the country gentleman, to whom they still look up, though many say they hate him with an irreconcilable hatred. Where there are no country gentlemen the peasant seems to be absolutely ruined. The fact is, the entire population is invertebrate. The country gentleman has been placed in a most unaviable position. The peasants believe that the Tzar has given him money for distribution, and that he is keeping it back. If this view gains ground it may lead to very serious complications.

A curious incident, which occurred the other day, illustrates the prevailing feeling and the attitude of the peasants, who regard relief in many cases as a right. A party of peasants went to a telegraph station and handed in a telegram addressed to the Emperor, to the effect that the governor of the province was stealing the money which was their due, and which "The Little Father" had sent for distribution amongst them. The telegram was not sent, but it led to an inquiry, which proved that a belief existed amongst the people that, as they sent their money to the Emperor, it was his duty to feed them. Besides, it was thought that as he could have as much money as he liked, money could be no object to him.

Should the patience of the peasant give out, the country gentleman will be the first to feel the effects of his wrath. In the majority of cases the latter fails to realise his danger, and is assuming bullying airs and despotic ways now that famine has again placed the peasants in his power. The foolishness of this attitude is obvious. I asked my guide, as we were driving along, how the peasants behaved, and said that I found them very humble and respectful. "Yes," he said, "that is what we are trying to make them again. They had become too independent and insolent, but we hope the Zemski Natchalniki will alter all that."

I was presently to have an instance of the altered condition of things.

"That village over there," said my friend, "is comparatively well off. Those are Government peasants—that is to say, they have no land of their own, but are tenants of the Government."

"I should like to see one or two of their huts, if I may, by way of contrast."

"Certainly," he said; and we drove up.

It is perhaps as well to preface what follows by pointing out that the Government peasants had never been the serfs of the country gentlemen, consequently they had no feeling of personal loyalty towards them, and, as they were not suffering from the famine, they had no object in assuming a virtue they did not possess.

We marched into the first hut with the same want of ceremony with which we had entered the others, but we were received very differently. A handsome woman, with laughing eyes and clean face, was playing the hostess, and was presiding at a well-scoured table over a very substantial repast of pancakes, cabbage, soup and porridge. Round the table sat about seven or eight women, of different degrees of cleanliness, all apparently in the best of humours, and enjoying thoroughly the hospitality of their hostess. The hut, or rather cottage, was built of brick. It had a deal floor. The door was covered with felt, the interior was clean, and the air comparatively pure. I could quite imagine a wholesome animal life in a cottage such as this.

"Show us your bread," said my friend.

"Isvoltye" (if you please), replied the self-satisfied hostess, as she smilingly showed us her excellent bread; "but why do you want to see it?" she asked; "we have not asked for help yet, but you will not pass us over if we want it, will you, sir?"

"What cattle have you got? Let us see your sheep and cows," said my friend.

Here an uneasy feeling seemed to come over her. I thought I could see the fear working in her mind that the well-filled barns and sleek cattle her husband possessed might be forcibly taken away from her to help to feed the less fortunate.

"I beg your pardon, sir, but it's a very cold day, sir; need I come with you, sir?" she asked.

"Then let your son show us over the cattle shed and barns," said my friend, so she sent her son, an obstinate, sturdy young fellow of about eighteen. We came to a pen full of sheep.

"How many sheep have you?"

"I don't know," said the boy, surlily; "count them yourself, there they are."

"Oh," said my guide, "is that the way you answer when you are spoken to? Go and report yourself under arrest."

The mother, who suspected something was wrong, now came running out, and, on ascertaining what had occurred, began pleading her son's cause, but my friend was inexorable.

As we went away, the woman shouted after us, "There they go. They take pleasure in looking at the misery of the poor, and go about inspecting us. Much good they do!"

The picture is complete. From trembling, starving paupers, hoping to get aid, to well-fed, wealthy peasants, who did not want any, all hated the gentleman, the man who wore a German coat and a white shirt, the "Barin."

"How about that young fellow whom you ordered to report himself under arrest?" I asked my guide. "What will happen if he does not obey you?"

"Oh, then he will be fetched, and get three days' imprisonment. If he reports himself, he will only get one."

"But what power have you behind you to enforce your authority?"

"The Zemski Natchalnik."

"What power has he?"

"He is everything; he is a little king."

"Perfectly, but how can he enforce his authority? Has he police, or are there any troops near?"

"Oh, yes, there are police, but we do not want them. The peasants know they have to do as they are told."

"To-day," he continued, "you saw the peasants under the most favourable conditions;

to-day is Sunday, and yesterday the whole of Russia washed. To-day Russia may be said to be clean." If that was what they were like when they were clean, I thought, I did not wish to see them when they were dirty.

CHAPTER V.

COUNT TOLSTOI'S KITCHENS.

It was in a little cottage standing alone in a clearing, which was once the heart of a great forest, that I took leave of the prince and his friends who had entertained me so hospitably, and shown me so much. The weather, as I resumed my journey through the Province of Riasan, was intensely cold, the thermometer at 21 degrees Réamur, while a keen wind was blowing in my teeth. I was wrapped up in a dokha, a deer-skin coat lined with fur, which neither wind nor cold could penetrate. I had lived in this enormous garment, which made me look twice my natural size, for several days, and I felt and smelt like an animal. My face was hung with icicles, and my feet, which I had not yet provided with the very necessary valenki, or felt over-shoes, soon lost all sensation. My driver was wrapped in two sheep skins, and the horses were perfectly white with frost. In this condition, the wind blowing in our teeth, we drove and drove for hours. I lost all consciousness of time and space, and was trying hard to forget the cold.

Suddenly my driver stopped in a village, and announced that he had lost his way. Here was a situation. It was almost as bad as being out at sea in a small sailing boat without a compass. We finally succeeded in routing out a peasant, who, taking full advantage of our case, exacted an exorbitant price for taking us to our destination. I went into his hut to warm myself while he was getting his horse and sledge ready. The dwelling was comparatively comfortable, a sufficient supper was spread upon the table, and a well-fed peasant, with fierce, bushy whiskers, eyed me suspiciously, while the women huddled themselves together in a corner. I resolved to maintain an entirely neutral attitude, not wishing to run any risks by interrogating the suspicious natives on my own account. Notwithstanding my caution, however, I soon found myself the subject of distrustful cross-questionings.

"I suppose you are connected with the Red-Cross Society?" said the peasant.

It was so easy to acquiesce, and so difficult and risky to explain what I really was, that I answered in the affirmative.

"Will they soon send us money?" he continued.

My heart was moved with pity.

"Yes," I said, "very soon. I am going try to to make them send it as soon as possible."

"God help you," said the peasant moodily. "We have waited patiently, and suffered long enough. God grant that help may come soon."

By this time, the man who was going to be

our guide appeared, carefully muffled up, and I got into my sledge. The peasant's sledge, driven by one horse, led the way. It looked like a little speck as it dived into the dales, and ascended the hillocks of snow that lay in our path. In solemn procession we thus drove through the starry night. It was eerie work. I was quite unarmed. The peasant thought I belonged to the Red-Cross Society, and carried money. My driver knew that I had money, for I paid him from day to day. What was I to do if they were to take it into their heads to rob me? But the Russian peasant is, on the whole, fairly honest. He may pilfer, but he seldom robs. At last our guide lost his way also. Fortunately we soon afterwards stumbled upon a village, and the Elder came out and directed us.

It was a strange experience, driving through those silent villages in the dead of night. The huts are generally built on each side of an enormous road, and stand lost and lonely in a wide expanse of snow-covered ground. The scene was at once romantic and depressing.

I had parted from my newly-made friends at seven in the evening. It was midnight before I reached my destination. I was received cordially by the Zemski Natchalnik, to whom I had been recommended. Supper was over, but an impromptu one was got ready for me. My host was a nervous, earnest man, of much learning, but few years. His mother-in-law spoke English, and his children had French and German governesses to each them the languages of the west.

"Properly speaking, there is no actual starvation at present, but it will come," he said, thoughtfully. "There is much distress, and great difficulty in aiding the peasants. We do not wish to distribute alms indiscriminately, and hence many perplexities and troubles arise."

I have already hinted at the difficulty of accurately estimating the true condition of the peasants. This springs from many causes. First among these, is the untrustworthiness of the peasants themselves. They know that help is being given, and they naturally try to get some for themselves, without much regard to the question whether they are in want of it or not. They argue that they have paid their taxes, and that, therefore, it is the duty of the Tzar to feed them. They hide their stores of grain and flour, tell ficititous tales, and always state that they have been three days without food. How is a Zemski Natchalnik, or one of the unofficial patrons of the peasants or guardians of the poor, to accurately gauge the degrees of distress amongst the peasants of his district? The Zemski Natchalnik has, on an average, a population of 100,000 souls under his charge. It is manifestly impossible to investigate each case; hence it is easy to impose upon him. The peasant is seldom in what may be called affluent circumstances in the best of years, and it is not easy for those who are accustomed to see him year by year nearly on the verge of starvation, to say whether he is exceptionally badly off or not. He is so hardy, and can keep alive on so little, that he does not soon show the effects of "short commons" in his face; nor is it easy to say, from the storage of food he may possess, how long he will be able to support life. The length of time a Russian peasant's family can support themselves upon a few mouldy crusts, is one of those problems that perplex the mind. Absolute starvation is the only condition upon which relief is distributed. Naturally, the peasant, in these circumstances, exaggerates the urgency of his need.

The chief difficulty, however, in arriving at an estimate of the real state of affairs, is the great gulf that exists between the gentry and the peasantry.

Sitting in the study of my new host, I found a curious-looking man. He had come on business, and was one of the few persons who had endeavoured to bridge over the chasm between the upper and lower classes in rural Russia, to which I have just alluded. He was at one time a common peasant, but had risen by his own efforts, and is now manager of M. Royeffski's estate, upon which Count Tolstoi has been carrying on his philanthropic work. I observed that this man had the lofty and vaulted brow of a thinker, and the eyes of an enthusiast. He seemed about fifty years of age. Perhaps he is the most interesting man I have yet come across. He had the broadest and most cultured views. He had evidently studied political economy, and it soon became clear, from his conversation, that there were very few subjects he did not know something about. He was remarkably shrewd, and had an original way of expressing himself, which betrays humour and common sense. He cordially invited me to come over the following morning to see Count Tolstoi's work. Next morning, my host's house was fairly stormed by peasants.

There were about 200 of them collected in front of the modest mansion. They were admitted in lots of about half-a-dozen, and my friend asked them what they wanted. It was always the same tale; they wanted food. Some wanted to be put on the list for relief; others came to complain that their names had been taken off.

My friend reasoned with them.

"How are you to be believed? Trofim told me a pitiable story, and then I found out he was lying. You know Trofim does not deserve help."

"Oh, yes," the peasants chimed in; "Trofim certainly does not want help."

"Then how are we to tell? I will see what I can do for you."

"Please, sir," said one man, "you got my wife and children permission to go to the free dinners, and now they have been sent back and refused."

These were Count Tolstoi's free dinners.

"Oh, have they? That is all right. I must inquire into that. I expect you have been shamming like the rest. We must see whether you are in need of relief at all."

The peasant addressed looked crestfallen.

Numerous others came to complain that the grain which was being distributed by the Zemstvo had not yet arrived.

"Well," said the Natchalnik, "you must wait a little more. Try to bear a little longer."

It was terrible advice to have to give. The man looked ashamed of himself as he gave it.

Before I left him he said, "We expect to be pillaged and burnt down before the spring, but what are we to do? Our own case is desperate. If it had not been for the potatoes this year, I don't know what I should have done. All my other crops have failed, and I actually had to buy seed for sowing."

I had looked forward with pleasurable anticipations to my visit to M. Royeffski's estate. His country house was small and humble, like most of the country residences I had seen in this district. It did not stand separate and alone, like the houses of other country gentlemen, but at the end of a large and populous village. The manager, whom I had met on the previous evening, received me. He took me into a small room, about ten feet by five. A small iron bedstead occupied the length of one wall. Near the window stood a rough writing-table. There was a small shelf of books. The room was destitute of anything approaching to ornament, and, of course, there was not the vestige of a carpet or curtains, or any of the appurtenances of English comfort. "This," said my guide, "is the sacred chamber. Here the great man lives and works. This is Count Tolstoi's room when he is here. I occupy it in his absence. Well, now, let us go and get something to eat," he said. "Do you eat eggs? You see we have no meat."

An enormous dish of fried eggs which was prepared, I devoured with the voracity of an ogre. There were staying in the house two disciples of Count Tolstoi — young men of education and culture in the garb of peasants. One was an uncommunicative giant, who sat and stared at me with anything but benevolence. The other, a small, nervous young man, with sparkling little eyes, entertained me with most interesting talk. His view was evidently this—that people should have the courage of their opinions, and act out in their lives the convictions of their hearts.

"We are suffering from a want of ideals," he said. "We must bravely act up to the precepts of our religion to restore them. The Middle Ages produced people who were not afraid of a martyr's death. How is it that there are no martyrs now!" He had a great contempt for the weak-kneed Liberals who valued their salaries more than their principles, and he had no faith in the modern doctrine of sitting down and waiting for an evolution of history. He seemed to think that men made history, and that in the absence of men of character and courage there could be no historical growth. His views were a curious mixture of primitive Christianity, Carlyle, and Ruskin.

We now proceeded to inspect M. Royeffski's village. It was about dinner time for the peasants, and so we entered one of those improvised eating-houses, in which Count Tolstoi feeds the people at the rate of 3s. a head per month. The ordinaries—there were several — were generally kept by some particularly destitute widow or very poor family. The woman of the house, in exchange for her services in cooking the food, received her own meals and fuel free, and was delighted with the bargain. In the one we entered there were only women and children. They were eating cabbage soup and excellent bread, not three-quarters potato, like the bread to which even the country gentlemen were reduced. We were asked to sit down and eat. "It is excellent food," the people round us exclaimed in chorus. "God bless the good Count and all his friends for giving us such good meals. What should we have done without him? We never want to eat better food than this." As we left the hut, touched with the evident sincerity of these simple creatures, the woman to whom the hut belonged came out with us.

"You see this roof," she said; "the Count had it built for me. I had been obliged to burn mine down for fuel, and don't know what would have become of us, if the good Count had not helped us."

This little incident shows at once the touching childishness, the improvidence, and the simplicity of the Russian peasant. What other rational human being would have burned the roof over his head, in order to keep himself warm? It is like pawning one's clothes to buy a night-shirt. But the peasant has a perfectly childish trust in the future. "Avos," the Russian word, inadequately expressed by the English "mayhap," is the constant comfort and solace of millions of the Tzar's subjects.

I visited several other ordinaries, and in a few I found men. But I was informed that men were rather ashamed of going to these ordinaries, and preferred to send their wives and children. Only those who felt the pinch of hunger too deeply to consider pride and self-respect, accepted this form of charity. Everywhere the Count's name was blessed. "Every day," said a woman, fervently, "we pray God to bless the Count, and return thanks for his benefits." The peasantry in this village struck me as being much less distrustful, and more honest, than in any I had yet visited.

On our way back, we met numbers of little boys, carrying books. They were coming from the village school, founded by the Count, and now captured by the local priest. The boys looked bright and truthful, as healthy boys should, and showed us their books with fearless frankness. It was evident, from all I saw, that Count Tolstoi, with his doctrines of Christian love and tolerance, is exercising an influence of the most powerful kind upon these simple folk.

CHAPTER VI.

AN INTELLECTUAL CENTRE.

When I mentioned to people that I was going to Voronesh, they invariably remarked, "Oh, Voronesh, an intellectual town—a very intellectual town!" So far as my experience of the place has gone, this characterisation is fairly well justified. When I arrived there, I found that the Zemstvo, or Local Government Council, was in session, and I attended several of its meetings. I had introductions to one or two members of this august body, and in the course of a few hours I had been introduced to all the leading local magnates.

The Zemstvo of Voronesh, if less imposing, is certainly more business-like than that of Tula. The President, M. Venevitinoff, who is also the marshal of nobility, comes of a literary family, and is himself well-known as an archæologist of authority and learning. His wife, who is a daughter of the famous Prince Stcherbatoff, one of the fathers of the Zemstvo, speaks English perfectly. She takes a keen interest in the question of local government, and regularly attends the meetings over which her husband presides, listening with almost passionate earnestness to the debates. M. Venevitinoff does not preside in uniform, but wears the simple frock coat of modern civilisation, on the breast of which, however, no decorations are displayed. His manner is easy and business-like. The other members are quite as simple, and very thorough. Business is the order of the day, and the Zemstvo of Voronesh has been very thoroughgoing and practical. It has spent large sums in buying corn, it has exerted itself to a remarkable degree, and it is in a position to say that, come what may, the peasants of the province of Voronesh need not die of starvation. A member of the Zemstvo told me that the first intimation he had had of a famine was from the Government itself last July. The Government summoned the Zemstvo to hold extraordinary meetings, and at these the Governors-General of the respective provinces read messages from the Government, announcing that a general famine might be expected, and that the Zemstvo must take measures to meet this national calamity. My informant told me that he had indeed been aware that the crops had failed in his own district, but he little dreamed that a general famine was imminent. In August, of course, everybody knew.

Nevertheless, the province of Voronesh has suffered terribly. In many villages the majority of the huts are deserted, the peasants preferring to seek in other climes that subsistence which their native land refuses to yield them. Siberia is a favourite field for emigration. The death-rate has increased 100 per cent.

and marriages have almost entirely ceased. It is needless to say that the peasant ceased this year to sing and get drunk on his holidays as he used to do, and consequently the receipts of the wine-shops in this province have already declined by 25 per cent. Voronesh is one of the wealthiest provinces of Russia, and in ordinary years when you drove into a village, it was impossible to see the huts of the peasants for the stacks of corn which they had piled around them. This year there are no piles of corn to be seen at all. The peasants have even taken their palings to pieces and sold them. It is estimated that 45 per cent. of the horses and cattle of the peasantry have been sold and lost to the country, because the majority were in so bad a condition that they could only be sold to the knackers. The average price of these half-starved animals has been about 6s. The price of good serviceable horses, on the other hand, has risen enormously. The town of Voronesh is infested with beggars of all descriptions, whose haggard looks and diffident manner seem to testify to the genuineness of their distress. They are all supposed to be starving peasants. The townspeople have formed themselves into a gigantic benevolent society. Charitable theatrical performances take place every evening to crowded houses, and the ladies have organised free bakeries and free kitchens. The Venevitinoffs have a free bakery on their estate, as well as in the town. Ladies' visiting committees are organised, and work of a most energetic character is going on everywhere.

All this public activity is a most welcome sign, and there are not wanting thinkers who maintain that the famine, so far from being a calamity, is a blessing in disguise, and may cause an awakening of public opinion and rouse society to a proper sense of its duties. There are in Voronesh, as everywhere else, many different opinions as to the state of the country, but the more earnest men whom I have spoken to seem to be fairly unanimous upon several points. It is quite clear, for instance, that the present condition of the peasantry is anything but satisfactory. The peasantry have increased and multiplied since 1858 to the extent of 40 per cent., but their land has not been improved. Instead of increasing in productiveness, it has actually deteriorated. This is due largely to the primitive agricultural methods of the peasant, and to the fact that he is exhausting the soil without putting anything into it, and also to the reckless destruction of forests which has been going on during the last twenty-five years. On the one hand the productiveness of the soil has declined, on the other hand the price of corn has fallen. Foreign competition is ruining the Russian grain trade. Whether this is due to the dishonesty of the Russian corn merchants, as some maintain, or whatever the cause may be, Europe, and especially Great Britain, is learning to do without Russian grain. This decline in the Russian grain trade makes itself felt in all other branches, and leads many Russian thinkers to ponder over the wisdom of protection. If Russia wishes to shut herself off from Europe, she must learn to do without European customers. While, then, Russian trade is declining in every branch, the condition of the peasant is not improving. Nothing is being done to raise his status. I ventured to express the opinion to a member of the Zemstvo that the peasant should have been raised to a sense of self-reliance and self-help, instead of being placed under the guardianship of fussy Zemski Natchalniki.

"My dear sir," said the gentleman, "you are quite right, but that would be against the fundamental principle of the autocracy in this country. We have neither law, nor order, nor self-respect, nor independence. There is nothing but the will of the Tzar; and the Zemski Natchalniki are the interpreters of the Tzar's will to the people, and the mediators between the people and the Tzar. You know the peasant has no fundamental conception of law. He believes that every country gentleman holds his land at the pleasure of the Emperor, and that the land we possess has been practically stolen from the people. That is the popular idea."

The peasant considers it the duty of the Government to feed him, and hence there is considerable danger of his becoming quite demoralised, and refusing to work. I am told that the gentry in this province are very nervous about the peasantry, and expect a sort of Jacquerie in the spring. The gunsmiths of Voronesh say they have never done so brisk a trade as this year, and that their shops have been completely cleared out. There is no solidarity between gentleman and peasant. In my opinion, the Mir is to blame for this. It is an institution by means of which Russian statesmen have thought pauperism would be prevented. But a communal system of land tenure has serious drawbacks, which go far to outweigh its obvious advantages. The Government have made agricultural labourers, as a class, impossible. The gentry, consequently, are directly interested in keeping the entire peasantry in a low state of economic development, in order to keep down the market value of their labour. I am told that one of the great fears of the landed gentry is that the peasant may become too prosperous to work for them at a rate of wages sufficiently low to make farming profitable. This is a lamentable state of affairs.

Another deplorable circumstance is the absolute want of skilled labour, technical knowledge, and practical education. The Germans and foreigners who used to be the foremen and estate agents and engineers of Russia, have been gradually turned out during the last ten years, and there is nobody to take their place. The Government does not discourage technical education on principle, but it is gradually closing the technical schools of the empire, because the pupils have proved insubordinate, and susceptible to revolutionary propaganda. This policy is very much like refusing to use a steam boiler, because steam boilers are liable to explode, especially when they are not provided with safety valves. The consequence is a dearth of engineers and agriculturists, which is very keenly felt. In the meantime, the agriculture of Russia is declining, the rivers are becoming shallow and sandy, and the railways are neglected. I am told there is a scheme to build a fourth railway to the Volga from the line Ryasan-Gryazi. There are three already; while the enormous square, Oriel - Koursk - Kharkoff - Ekaterinoslavl and Kasan-Samara-Saratoff-Astrakhan, is absolutely unconnected by railways. Yet this is the great grain country of Russia. There is a scheme on foot for building a railway from Penza, *via* Voronesh, to Kharkoff, the importance of which cannot be over-estimated. The Volga is one of the natural highways of Russia, but is, unfortunately, frozen over during the greater part of the year. It would seem natural and imperative that the great grain centres of Kazan, Samara, and Saratoff should not be dependent upon the weather for their export trade, but should be connected by railway with Novotcherkask or Taganrog. All these are questions which require to be dealt with by experts and practical men. But these seem to be absolutely wanting. The engineers and technical men of Russia have an evil reputation, and are certainly not more honest or less self-seeking than other officials. Every one seems to regard the country as a company promoter is supposed to regard the public in England—as something to plunder.

My stay in Voronesh has been made very pleasant for me. I am sorry to leave this intellectual centre, but I must hurry on to the scenes of distress and privation. I have invitations from several country gentlemen in the province, and hope to obtain, through their kindness, much valuable information as to the state of the country.

CHAPTER VII.

THE VILLAGES OF VORONESH.

IN the course of my journeyings through the various villages and country districts of Russia I have been entirely dependent for food and shelter upon the hospitality of country gentlemen to whom I had been recommended. Each stopping place was reached after a long and cheerless drive across immense tracts of snow-covered country, whose level monotony was broken only at long intervals by a few trees, a village, or a piece of rising ground. Lest people should form a wrong idea of what stopping in the country houses of Russian gentlemen means, and imagine that I have been nursed in the lap of luxury during my journey, I will describe the mansion of one of my hosts, from which some conception of the average Russian country house may be obtained. It was a low one-storeyed log-house, standing alone in a bleak wilderness of snow. It had two fairly large rooms and three smaller ones. The deal floors were uncarpeted, the walls were unpapered, the furniture was primitive and scanty, and we all slept where we could. My host gave me an iron bedstead, with a mysterious mattress full of inequalities of surface, he himself slept on three chairs, while another guest occupied a horse-hair sofa—by the way, all in one room. Our toilettes even were matters of form. A tub was out of the question, and washing a perfunctory ceremony. In every instance, however, I was most hospitably entertained, and was afforded every possible facility for investigating the distress.

Where the gentry are housed, fed, and even clothed little better than peasants it is not extraordinary that the peasants should live like savages.

I have in mind a venerable peasant who has a family of thirteen, amongst them married sons and daughters, with their wives and husbands and children, and they all live in one wretched little hut and sleep in a sort of heap on the stove. When you enter a peasant's hut you see three or four women doing domestic work, generally, in Voronesh, weaving clothing for themselves and their family. In the domestic economy of a peasant's family the women find the clothing, the men the food and taxes. The earnings of the unmarried girls are not touched, but go towards making up a "portion." Well, as you enter a peasant's hut, you find the women sitting about engaged in some work, but as you get inside and begin to be able to discern objects more clearly in this smoke-laden atmosphere, you see little heads peeping anxiously down upon you from the top of the stove, and you gradually realise the fact that on the top of that stove there lies an undiscovered country, little dreamt of even by educated Russians themselves. It is quite impossible to obtain even an approximate idea of the life on that stove, with its tragedies and comedies. We know as little of it as we do of the lives of the cockroaches who share that stove with its legitimate occupants. The peasant cannot induct us into the mysteries of that life. To him it is neither mysterious nor extraordinary. The educated peasant who has risen in life, and there are a few such, will never reveal its horrors. The only side-light which is occasionally thrown upon it comes from the law courts. Frequently peasants are tried for murdering their fathers, and generally the motive is jealousy. The sturdy young peasant who goes into the town to earn a little money during the winter, leaves his young wife behind him in his father's hut. The latter very frequently prefers his youthful daughter-in-law to the aged mother of that daughter-in-law's husband, and hence terrible tragedies arise. These occurrences are so common that the Russian language has actually a special term for such a father. Thirty years ago the peasant was the cattle of the neighbouring gentleman, and as such was looked after by him, and kept from want because this was the gentleman's interest. For more than a generation the peasant has ceased to be the property of the neighbouring gentleman; he has been converted into the property of the Government. As long as he remained in his herd or village commune, paid his taxes, and kept quiet, that Government took no notice of him. But, after a time, it was discovered that the sacred gift of liberty had not proved the boon which it was supposed to be. The peasant is generally admitted to have degenerated since his emancipation. Nothing had been done to educate him; nothing had been done to awaken in him a feeling of self-reliance and independence. He remained the serf he had been, with this difference, his master was away. Hence the appointment of guardians, or Zemski Natchalniki, to take the place of the master who has gone. We have seen in a former chapter that it is against the principle of the autocracy to raise the peasant above the condition of a brute beast, to give him a sense of justice, to educate and enlighten him. In Russia there is no law outside the autocrat's will, as interpreted by his officials; no independence, no self-respect. Those who have ventured to bring a sort of moonshine of enlightenment among the peasantry have been sent to Siberia.

The peasantry in the Government of Voronesh, which is one of the most important grain-growing districts in Russia, have hitherto been comparatively prosperous. Many of them live in huts which bear a greater resemblance to labourers' cottages in England than any I have yet seen since I entered the famine-stricken region. These dwellings are built of red brick; pretty designs in white stone, representing columns, arches, and the like, being let into the walls. Here, however, as everywhere else, the most terrible contrasts present themselves, and the peasants' huts are even more dilapidated and wretched than those I saw in Riasan. Many of them have no chimneys. The interiors of these look as if they had just received a coating of pitch, and are pervaded by a strong odour of tar arising from a soot deposit which accumulates year after year without ever being disturbed. It is said that the peasants who live in these murky hovels are exceedingly healthy, but upon inquiry I discovered that their eyesight frequently suffers from the constant irritation which the smoke engenders.

It is by no means easy to convey an accurate impression as to the actual condition of the province I have just traversed. That the distress is real and urgent admits of no doubt whatever. But there are bright spots and dark spots, and detailed descriptions of either or both are apt to be misleading. I have, however, been able to get hold of some statistical information collected on the spot, which indicates more clearly and describes more eloquently than any number of fine phrases or random statements the position of certain districts in relation to their food supply.

To begin with, there are in the province of Voronesh six extensive parishes, whose harvest returns this year were 20 per cent., not below, but of, the average. The Volost of Beresovo has a population (not including infants under two years old) of 9233. Its harvest this year amounted to 14,882 poods of rye and 8385 poods of all other kinds of grain. The communal grain reserve amounted to 5580 poods, and the rich peasants' private grain reserve to 15,894 poods. Thus the total resources of the Volost to feed a population of some 10,000 souls throughout the winter—not to speak of horses and cattle—were represented by 44,741 lbs. of grain. To realise what this means you have only to divide the number of poods by 9233, and you will find that there was a food supply of less than five poods, or 180 lbs., per head of the population for the entire winter. The normal consumption of black bread by a peasant family is about 3 lbs. per head per day, and it follows that, but for public and private charity, the population of the Volost would at the present moment be without a crumb to eat.

The following figures, for which I am indebted to M. Ertel, the novelist, are still more eloquent. They relate to the village of Makari, the provisioning of which he has undertaken on his own account. He has managed to collect contributions amounting to £100 a month, and these he is administering with an unselfishness and application deserving the highest praise. To a literary man, especially a novelist without private means, time is money. Yet M. Ertel devotes the whole of his mornings to the reception of peasants and the distribution of relief. I saw as many as 200 applicants relieved in the course of a single forenoon. Every one received the fullest attention, and every case was carefully investigated. M. Ertel has made a record of the circumstances of each peasant, and was thus able to check his story. Particularly heartrending were the numerous cases of widows and deserted wives.

Here is an abstract of M. Ertel's statistics. The parish of Makari embraces seven villages, which contain among them 254 courts or families, representing a total population of 1532 persons. Of these there are at the present moment in a condition of absolute want 200 families, comprising 559 children and 560 adults, in all 1119 souls out of a population of 1532. Fifty-eight of these destitute families have no live stock of any description; 39 have a cow or a pig, but no horse; while 86 still have one horse, and 17 have two. Since September last more than half the live stock in these villages has been sold or killed. Here is M. Ertel's tabulated statement:—

	Sept. 1891.	Dec. 1891.
Horses	225	153
Cows	203	145
Sheep	966	382
Pigs	95	27
Total	1489	707

Such is the condition to which a once-prosperous parish has been reduced. It is fortunate in having been made the especial care of a gentleman whose literary reputation has enabled him to become the disburser of numerous liberal subscriptions. I found staying at his house M. Potapenko, one of the most successful and most promising of Russia's young novelists, who had come down into the district to found free dinners.

Not far from Makari lies a village which is in a very much worse plight, because there the same amount of charitable aid has not been forthcoming. It is called Orlova. With a population of 6000 souls, it has no one to look after it but a priest, whose resources are so slender that any relief he is able to distribute is a mere drop in the ocean. I was assured that cases of death from starvation had actually occurred in that village. These, however, I could not stay to investigate.

The situation in Makari and Orlova strikingly illustrates two of the great disadvantages against which Russia now labours. The first is the disappearance of the old wealthy landed proprietors, with no one to take their place; the second is the tendency the peasants have of crowding together in large villages, while their land is distributed frequently at a considerable distance. There are some cases of peasants living at a distance of ten miles and more from their land. The present agricultural system is altogether a hopeless failure. Everything points to the fact that the peasant is quite incapable of looking after himself. The village commune hangs like a millstone round his neck, and hampers all his efforts, such as they are, to get on.

A very different picture is presented on the estate of her Imperial Highness the Princess Eugenie, of Oldenburg, near the village of Ramon. Here wealth, benevolence, and sound judgment go hand in hand. Ramon is a sort of centre of sweetness and light, whose rays are felt by the peasants within a radius of even one hundred miles. Ramon is a standing argument in favour of the existence of large estates. It supports a sugar factory employing 2400 hands, a carpet-weaving establishment, a hospital, and in the summer its fields give employment to numbers of peasants. The Princess is herself an artist of no mean ability, and conducts, besides, scientific experiments of considerable interest on plants. Her manager, M. Klingen, is a Russian, of German extraction, with remarkable energy and great skill. He is a meteorologist of repute, and his observations upon the snowfall of the country are considered unique. His researches confirm the views of Professor Stebut, and help to prove the importance to Russia of planting lines of forest on her eastern frontier to protect her from the devastating east winds to which she is subject, and which drive away her snow. Snow is wealth to Russia. When the thaw sets in this snow is converted into manure, and makes her fields fruitful. M. Klingen maintains that Russia should protect her fields by means of natural barriers of trees of different sizes, planted in the shape of a pyramid. Another important discovery made by this gentleman shows the inventiveness of his mind. He has found that the refuse of sugar beet, thrown out by his factory, not only makes a capital manure and a splendid food for cattle, but, when mixed in proper proportion with rye, adds considerably to the digestibility of rye bread. By careful experiments upon himself, his own family, and finally upon the workmen in his factory, he satisfactorily established this last conclusion, and now bakes large quantities of bread mixed with the refuse of sugar beet. This bakery gives employment to a large number of hands, besides keeping down the market price of bread generally. His bread is eagerly sought by adjacent peasantry, who throng his bakery all day. He finds he cannot bake fast enough to supply the demand.

The Ramon Hospital and Dispensary is free, and a model of cleanliness. This is also visited by peasants living at a great distance, and record is kept of every patient. It was here that I first realised one of the primary difficulties in the way of free public dinners. Russian peasants eat together out of one common dish with a wooden ladle, which passes from hand to hand and mouth to mouth. Thus any one suffering from the contagious skin diseases which are so common in that country might easily infect a whole village. As it is, the peasantry of Russia are decimated by this modern scourge. Ramon is most picturesquely situated on the top of a hill, at whose base flows the river Don. On the other side lie extensive forests. These forests have saved the people of the neigbourhood from severe privation. The peasants are allowed to collect firewood for themselves in the woods this year. Another very important institution in Ramon is its school. Illiteracy is the curse of the Russian peasant. There can be no doubt if there were more estates like Ramon the state of the people would be less pitiable than it is.

It is pleasant to come here and there upon bright spots in these dreary steppes. Another such is to be found at the village of Kon Kolodetz, thus called after a horse which belonged to Peter the Great, and which brought that monarch safe and sound to the banks of the Don after he had lost his way in the dense forests with which the country was then covered. The horse died from drinking the cold water of a spring in the neighbourhood, but its monument remains to tell the touching story. Here is the Zemstvo's School of Agriculture, maintained exclusively for the education of peasant children. Even here the hard times are felt, and the energetic head master told me the cattle on his model farm were getting thin and in poor condition from the scarcity and bad quality of their food. He also took me round the village, and there I saw pitiable pictures of poverty. It was dinner time, and the people were cooking their soup, which seemed little better than dirty, hot water. The men were wretched-looking, with hollow eyes, some in the last stages of fever, all huddled up on their horrible stoves, whither they had crawled to die. Here was an old woman, who was starving herself in order to feed her favourite boy, a selfish, impudent rascal of sixteen. There was another old woman whose husband had forsaken her, but who bravely struggled on with her family. The Zemstvo had just sent her some bread, and she was in great spirits. On her own showing, the bread would not last her more than three weeks, and she would not get a fresh loan for a couple of months, but she did not seem to be depressed. She was touchingly cheerful. Another family of twenty-five, all in one hut, comparatively well off, but living in the most horrible filth, seemed to be perfectly content, although they only ate every other day. One old woman told me she would eat a little bread, and then crawl back on her stove and try to forget the aches in her bones. In one hut that we entered I found an old woman trying to comfort two children, who were crying bitterly. "They want bread," she said, "and all I have to give them are these stale crusts, which they can't bite." While I was in another hut, a young fellow stumbled in pale and trembling, with large circles under his eyes. He was recovering from typhoid fever, but the scanty food and bad air prevented his getting well. Everywhere it was the same story. The marvel was that the people were not dead long ago. The peasant does not know how to economise his labour. He has no self-respect and no self-reliance, and but little industry. These virtues it is the object of the agricultural schools to teach. Unfortunately, these establishments are not numerous. The province of Voronesh, for instance, has only one, containing one hundred pupils. These are very naturally snapped up by the landed proprietors, and make capital stewards. It is only in the course of time that they will begin to leaven the peasantry.

Reviewing briefly the condition of Voronesh, it may be said that for the present no general starvation need be feared. The Zemstvo has made very complete arrangements. The Red-Cross Society is also very active, and private charity abounds. It is the future that troubles everybody. What will be the state of affairs in the spring and next year? Will the State be able to support the peasant much longer? Will the peasant himself start working, or will he not rather think that it is the Tzar's duty to feed him? Of course there will be public works, roads, and bridges, even railways; but what is to be done with those peasants who have sold their horses? When it was known that a famine had set in, certain benevolent and practical people arranged to have the horses and cattle of the peasants driven to the Caucasus, there to pasture until the spring, but the Government refused to sanction the scheme on the ground that to take away the peasants' horses, even temporarily, would be to deprive them of the means of earning money as carriers during the winter. Everybody is regretting now, when it is too late, that the scheme was not given effect to.

CHAPTER VIII.

TAMBOFF.

TAMBOFF is one of the smallest of the affected provinces. It has an area of 66,583 square kilometres, and a population of about two and a half millions. Its resources are entirely agricultural, there being no industries worth mentioning. The failure of the crops has therefore been severely felt, and, although no deaths from actual starvation have been reported, the dreaded hunger typhus has made its appearance in a certain number of villages. That the distress has not been more acute is mainly attributable to the prompt and energetic action of the Zemstvo, which not only saw that the fields were sown in due season, but made arrangements for a liberal distribution of relief. Already 7,000,000 roubles have been expended in provisioning the province. Situated as it is in the Steppes, Tamboff has no forests, and the peasants are suffering from the dearth of fuel quite as much as from lack of food. The chief difficulty in reaching and relieving the distress is the absence of means of communication.

I have just returned from a short visit to a Zemski Natchalnik resident about forty miles from this town. The villages through which I passed wore an appearance of comfort and cleanliness, such as certainly does not characterise those I saw in the provinces of Voronesh, Riasan, and Tula. The peasants I met were fine, strapping fellows; the women plump, rosy-cheeked, and gaily dressed, red being the predominant colour in their attire. In Tamboff the peasantry scorn to encase their feet in basket shoes; they wear boots and felt overshoes. Their sheepskins are also much smarter than those I saw in the other provinces. The men are tall, with handsome, regular features, fine eyes, and swarthy complexions. The women look happy and contented, but, I am told, are lamentably lax in their conduct. There is no doubt that Tamboff has hitherto been a prosperous province.

The Zemski Natchalnik, to whom I had a letter of introduction, received me with that matter-of-fact hospitality which is peculiarly Russian. There was no question of inviting me to stay; that was taken for granted.

My host had been a justice of the peace, and he regarded his new office as a distinctly reactionary institution, but he had accepted it for the simple reason, as he said, that if he did not take it some other fellow would. I found him a man of wide education and cultured tastes. One of his hobbies was a small stud, from which he managed to derive considerable profit. He told me that he sold about thirty horses annually, at an average price of £40. These horses are bought largely for St Petersburg and Moscow carriage work, though some find their way to Berlin. They are all of the famous Orloff breed—Arabs, crossed with Flemish and Dutch blood. They retain the fine coat and elegant head of the barb, but they lose the latter's cleanness of shape; they generally have clumsy legs and very poor hocks, but tremendous chests. A Russian dealer will not look at the slender feet of a barb; he wants substance.

At one time Tamboff was a great horse-dealing centre, but the country gentlemen have gradually reduced and abolished their studs, and only a few remain. This decline in one branch of country life is characteristic of all. It may be said that all along the line Russia has gone back. From an economic point of view, according to the popular belief, the emancipation of the serfs has been the curse of the country. This view is not confined to reactionary country gentlemen; it is the general opinion. Nothing has contributed more to the impoverishment of the country than the unscientific use which has been made of the railway system. Count Tolstoi, in the conversation I had with him in Moscow, said he could prove to me that the railways had ruined the country.

At that time I felt inclined to smile at this theory; but as I advanced in my journey through the distressed provinces, and hear the opinions of hard-headed, well-informed men of business, I cannot help feeling that there is a great deal to be said for Count Tolstoi's view.

The railways of Russia have been constructed largely with a view to the development of new grain-raising areas. They were run down to some fertile district, the land was worked on the American system, and exhausted, and then fresh grain areas were sought. The difference between the experience of America and that of Russia is this—in the former country the native population have been exterminated, in Russia they have been left to starve.

An agriculturist of authority told me that he had seen with his own eyes how the South Russian peasantry had been gradually sinking under the influence of the railway. Unable to compete with the large farmer, who came down from the north and exploited the land on a large scale, the native peasant was compelled to sell his oxen and his surplus land, and now he has only miserable little horses, too weak for the European plough, so he is obliged to content himself with a system of cultivation which amounts to little more than scratching the surface of the earth.

Before the advent of railways, the large proprietors could not profitably develop the resources of their estates. They turned only a very insignificant proportion into arable land, and they allowed the peasants to farm the rest at nominal rents. Then the peasant lived well and prospered. The transport trade was in his hands, and the neighbouring gentleman did not ruinously compete with him. But now the case is different. The railways have brought out the inequality between the peasant and the gentleman, and ruined the former without benefiting the latter, who, as a rule, squandered the wealth derived from his estate in Paris or at Monte Carlo. And now there is great lamentation all over the country because the whole of Russia is exhausted, with the exception of its last new territory, the Caucasus. The Caucasus is to-day what Samara was at a comparatively recent date, and what Little Russia was at an antecedent period; and so the process of exhaustion goes on.

This is what makes the condition of the peasant so deplorable. He is handicapped in every direction. On the one hand, he has for his competitors educated men, who have at their command the resources of modern science; on the other he is handicapped by his own ignorance, his many faults, his *mir*—which kills everything like individual enterprise—and his poverty in land; for the peasantry have increased in population since 1861 by 50 per cent. at least, but the land of the *mir* remains the same. A young Russian, with an original turn of mind, said to me: "Do you know why we love our *mir* so? If we had no *mir* the peasant would rapidly lose his land, and become an agricultural labourer. Then we should have to keep him all the year round. Now that he has land which would suffice to support him, if he had no taxes to pay, he is compelled to work for us for next to nothing." It may be that the peasant is not quite dependent upon the bounty of the gentlemen; still, the tendency of the system is in that direction.

But let us return to my Zemski Natchalnik, who discussed the situation with me in the frankest possible manner. "You see," he said, "it is extremely difficult to know how to help these peasants. There can be no doubt that they are really in great want. The harvest has been 20 per cent. of the average. It follows, therefore, that the thriftless peasant is in want. But there are numerous peasants who are not in want. For instance, the other day one came to me, fell on his knees, and entreated me to help him. He said he had not tasted food for three days, and his children were starving. When his case came to be investigated, it was discovered that he had buried large stores of flour under his hut."

My friend took me round the villages in his district, and the impression left upon my mind from this visit was that, at any rate, the peasants of Tamboff live less like pigs than their brethren in Voronesh and Riasan. Their distress seems also to be less acute. There were, of course, individual cases of great suffering; but, on the whole, the peasants seemed to be less destitute and less abject. All the huts that I have seen in this province present an appearance of cleanliness which contrasts pleasantly with the dirt and squalor of the central provinces. In some of the huts we found stores of stale crusts, on which the family hoped to exist for a week or so.

"Let us go to the village priest," said my guide; "he will interest you." I readily assented. The priesthood in Russia represent a sort of caste, and are the only independent estate in the country. Their attitude towards the peasants leaves much to be desired. The average village priest is often a drunkard—always uncultured, uneducated, unrefined. From whom is the unfortunate peasant to get his ideals? The gentleman, he distrusts; the priest, he hates; and neither the one nor the other is capable of exerting the proper sort of influence over him.

The village priest lived in a one-storey house, furnished very plainly. It was something better than a peasant's hut, and it was scrupulously clean. The priest himself was a consumptive-looking young man, with restless, cunning eyes, and a nervous manner; his wife was a stolid-looking person, little above the level of a peasant woman. The priest received us with marked courtesy. A visit from the Zemski Natchalnik was an honour indeed. We were offered tea and home-made biscuits, and remained some time. The priest came from Voronesh, and had but a poor opinion of Tamboff. "They are a self-indulgent, vain, and foolish people here," he said. "Some of them have nothing to eat, but they will wear red shirts and leather boots, and they keep their huts ridiculously clean." This was quite a new view of social ethics. The Zemski Natchalnik, in the course of conversation, told how a peasant had implored him for help. "As usual," he said, "the fellow had not tasted food for three days. I asked him where he was going. 'To the bazaar,' he answered. What are you going to do there?

I asked. 'I want to buy bark to make shoes,' the fellow replied. And yet he had not tasted food for three days! There is no relying upon anything they say."

"Oh! your honour," said the priest, "I wanted to ask you about some corn that I have. I have a few hundred pounds. Do you think the Zemstvo would buy it of me?"

"I will see about it," said the Zemski Natchalnik.

Here was a curious revelation! Before me stood the disciple of Christ, with long hair, pale face, cassock touching the ground, looking like a sacred picture. Round him was a starving people. And what was his dominant idea? The succour of the afflicted? The feeding of the hungry and the clothing of the naked? Nothing of the kind. His one concern was the price of the corn he had contrived to hoard. Yet this priest, the Zemski Natchalnik told me, was the best he had come across. I was even assured that many of the priests have not scrupled to accept their share of the Zemstvo's allotment of corn. In further conversation about the famine, the priest told us that a reverend brother in a neighbouring parish had sent a woeful story to the bishop concerning a peasant who had murdered his children because he was unable to feed them. The story proved to be an invention, but it served its purpose. The bishop was so horrified that he sent a considerable sum from the fund at his disposal for the relief of that particular village.

From the residence of the village priest we drove to that of the German steward on the Duke of Leuchtenburg's estate, Ivanovka. This gentleman has established free dinners for the poor, and has done a great deal to alleviate the distress in the neighbourhood. We had a most interesting conversation with him, and were hospitably entertained. We drove home by moonlight, our horses harnessed tandem on account of the narrowness of the snow tracks.

It was a curious and novel sensation driving tandem in a sledge, especially as the horses were not accustomed to this mode of harnessing, and the leader occasionally turned round and looked at us. The coachman had no whip, but managed the horses with his voice. Russian horses seem to understand perfectly what is said to them, and are marvellously obedient.

Next morning the Zemski Natchalnik gave a sort of audience to a number of peasants, and kindly allowed me to be present. A good many of the applicants came from one of the villages we had visited the day before to beg for bread, thinking I had brought money. Some wanted fuel, and received it from the Zemski Natchalnik's private store. An interesting case was that of a small boy of about fourteen, with clear, blue eyes, and a determined face.

"What do you want?" my host inquired.

"I want permission to go to Ekaterinodar."

"What do you want to do there?"

"I have a brother there, and he will find me work. I can get no work here, and I don't want to be a burden to my parents."

So the brave little fellow got his permission to leave the *mir*.

While my host was listening to the sorrows of the peasants, another guest arrived. It was Count Stroganoff's steward, a retired major of hussars, now close upon seventy, but as smart and dandified as a young fellow of twenty. Count Stroganoff has done a great deal for the peasants of his district, and has, indeed, taken their provisioning entirely upon himself, refusing all aid from the Zemstvo. His steward, Ivan Ivanovitch, had received his commission in 1848, and had been through the Hungarian campaign and the Crimean War. He was wounded at Balaclava, and gave me a vivid description of the historical charge of the Light Brigade.

"We were so sorry for them," he said;

"they were such fine fellows, and they had such splendid horses. It was the maddest thing that was ever done. I can't understand it. They broke through our lines, took our artillery, and then, instead of capturing our guns, and making off with them, they went for us. I had been in the charge of the Heavy Brigade in the morning, and was slightly wounded. We had all unsaddled, and were very tired. Suddenly, we were told, 'the English are coming.' 'Confound them,' we said. My colonel was very angry, and ordered his men to give no quarter. I was lying at some distance, with my wound bandaged, when I saw them coming. They came on magnificently. We thought they were drunk from the way they held their lances. Instead of holding them under their armpits, they waved them in the air, and, of course, they were easier to guard against like that. The men were mad, sir. They never seemed to think of the tremendous odds against them, or of the frightful carnage that had taken place in their ranks in the course of that long, desperate ride. They dashed in amongst us, shouting, cheering, and cursing. I never saw anything like it. They seemed perfectly irresistible, and our fellows were quite demoralised. We liked your fellows. When our men took prisoners they used to give them our *vodka*. Awful stuff it was!—more like spirits of wine than anything else. Your fellows used to offer us their rum in exchange, but we did not care for it; it was too soft and mild. The Russian soldier must have his *vodka!*"

CHAPTER IX.

THE GOLDEN PORT OF THE VOLGA.

SARATOFF used to be called "The Golden Port of the Volga." Since 1885, however, the river has rapidly receded from the once busy wharves, and now flows past at a distance of about three miles from the town to which it formerly bore wealth and prosperity. Between its present banks and the town proper, there now lies a wide expanse of sand, across which every summer a wooden bridge on trestles is erected, as a temporary means of communication for the people.

The gradual recession of the Volga from Saratoff is little short of a national calamity, for this river is the great natural highway of the Russian corn and timber trades. One of the most pressing wants of the district, therefore, one would imagine, is the regulation of this important channel, upon which so many material interests depend. But nothing is done in this direction. Indeed, the Government statist of the district, who ought to have some knowledge of political economy, informed me that it would really be easier and cheaper to build a fresh port than to regulate the course of this wayward current.

Yet Saratoff is a town with a population of 125,000, and is the terminus of a single line of railway, the journey over which occupies twenty-four hours. But Russia is a peculiar country.

Each province has its distinguishing characteristics. If Voronesh is a centre of intelligence; Tamboff, an old "noble's nest," which would have rejoiced the heart of Tourguenieff; Saratoff is essentially a mercantile centre. It is well built, with several excellent streets, which might challenge comparison with those of Moscow, or any continental city, and it possesses five bazaars. The last-mentioned fact alone speaks volumes for the commercial activity of this Russian inland Liverpool. But, notwithstanding its numerous population, its bazaars, its shops, and its railway, Saratoff, like the rest of Russia, goes to sleep during the winter.

I find that I have been preceded here by two English Quaker gentlemen, who visited several villages, and investigated the distress. There seems little doubt that the condition of the peasantry in this province is much more pitiable than that of their fellows in Central Russia, but I am told that the situation in Kazan is even worse than in Saratoff in respect of general destitution. What is felt most here is the absence of wealthy landowners. The old families have disappeared, and their places have been taken by merchants and corn exporters, who do not know the peasant, and do not care what becomes of him. The result is a state of affairs which is described as terrible. The Zemstvo has been less active than in other provinces. The late governor, General Kossitch, got into disfavour by speaking his mind too freely about the famine, and was obliged to retire. His influence, however, was so great that, instead of being made a member of the Supreme Council of the Empire, which is the Russian way of disgracing and shelving governors who commit indiscretions, he was promoted to the command of an army corps on the western frontier.

Saratoff has had considerable experience of famines, and the Zemstvo has every year to provide for a large proportion of the population. This annual assistance is given in the shape of loans, which the peasants have to refund under very disadvantageous conditions, for they are naturally made at times when corn, on account of its scarcity, commands famine prices, and repayment is exacted when an abundant harvest has brought about an exactly opposite state of affairs. But the peasant does not understand these economic laws, and looks upon the fluctuations of the market as being due to the machinations of the mercenary merchants. He knows that he receives a certain quantity of corn, and that, when he has to refund it, he is obliged to sell twice that quantity to obtain the requisite sum. This he regards as a cruel hardship.

The peasant has, perhaps, a better right to complain of the inefficient manner in which the relief is organised. If the present committees and official distributions had been suddenly called into existence by the famine, their shortcomings could be more easily explained, but, considered as established organisations, they exhibit in their operation an amount of friction and leakage that can only be deplored. Besides, the relief is hopelessly inadequate.

I arrived here in time to witness a great religious ceremony—the blessing of the waters of the Volga. It was a wonderful sight. In the background lay the town, the gilded cupolas of its churches glittering in the sun. On the frozen Volga was a curious little pagoda, somewhat resembling a small band-stand, and round it, about it, and stretching along the river on one side, and away up the town on the other, were dense crowds of people, mingled with whom were horses, sledges, and mounted police, the last-mentioned armed with whips, all squeezing and struggling, those on foot standing mostly knee-deep in snow. There were ladies in silk dresses, peasant women in their national costumes, and with gaily coloured shawls round their heads. At last there was a shout, and I could see, wending its way down the steep road which led to the river, a solemn procession of priests, conveying holy pictures and other emblems.

The procession was headed by the band of one of the infantry regiments of the garrison, then came men carrying banners and pictures. These were followed by the priests in gorgeous robes of cloth of gold. Presently the band ceased playing, and the air was rent by the chanting of a thousand voices. In thirty degrees of frost we stood, with heads bared, while the ceremony of blessing the water was performed inside the quaint little pagoda, underneath which the ice had been cut out. Fortunately, the ceremony did not last long. Next followed the blessing of the regimental flags of the garrison, and then there was a rush for the spot where the ice had been broken. Hundreds of young men flung their clothes in the snow, and jumped into the ice-cold water to wash away their sins. Judging from the anxiety manifested to go through this process, the sins must have been heavy and grievous. Just then the clock struck twelve, and the numerous factories which line the Volga blew their shrill steam whistles. Here was a strange contrast! On the one hand the priests, with their curious mediæval robes, the young men, shivering and naked, waiting for their turn to dip into the cold river; on the other, factories, railway trucks, and steam whistles.

When I came back to the town, I saw a crowd of ragged men, women and children standing in front of a small white house, and being kept in order by two policemen. They were German colonists come to receive alms, and the little white house was the palace of the Roman Catholic bishop of these unfortunate Germans. The bishop, to whom I was subsequently introduced, is doing a great deal of good amongst the poor, and has just opened a public ordinary, at which three hundred people are daily fed. The kitchen and dining-room for this ordinary have been fitted up by an Englishman, resident here—Mr John Golden, the engineer of the Saratoff Water Works, and the most popular man in the town. He and his energetic son do a great deal to alleviate the distress. He told me that it cost very little to help them. He had saved "a small neighbourhood" from starvation by distributing work and firewood, and by a total eleemosynary expenditure of about twelve shillings.

The general feeling amongst the citizens of Saratoff is one of indignation against the Red-Cross Society. The late governor, General Kossitch, collected hundreds of thousands of roubles, which were all sent to St Petersburg, and have neither been seen nor heard of since. The Red-Cross Society has established penny dinners, but that is all it has done as yet. Hence, the leading citizens have been compelled to take the question of providing for the starving peasants into their own hands. Herr Seiffert, one of the wealthiest residents, has opened free dinners at one end of the town, and similar ordinaries have been established elsewhere by the Lutheran pastor and others.

At first these efforts on the part of individuals were discouraged by the authorities. Herr Seiffert, for instance, was asked how many people he could feed, and how long he could feed them. He replied that he would feed as many as came, and would continue to do so as long as his means lasted. Then he was requested to make a list of the people he fed daily, with their names and addresses, and to send up this list to the governor every evening. This he declined to do, and he finally carried his point, and administers his own charity in his own way.

CHAPTER X.

SARATOFF ABORIGINES.

I HAVE have had some rather unpleasant experiences in trying to get at the distress in this province. To begin with, three days were lost in the vain endeavour to hire a troika. The cold was so intense that the yamstchiks refused to undertake a journey to remote rural districts. The thermometer showed 68 degrees of frost, and the cold was aggravated by biting winds. The schools were closed on account of the inclement weather, and the children were kept at home. In the streets of Saratoff huge fires were lighted, and round them clustered cabmen, peasants and others, whose calling kept them out of doors.

When I had at length succeeded in engaging a troika, I set out upon a visit to the Zemski Natchalnik of a district some thirty miles distant from this town. The journey was a most uncomfortable one. My driver was a phlegmatic German colonist, who could speak neither Russian nor German intelligibly. He drove so badly that the sledge was twice upset, and I was sent flying out into the snow. The horses were unyoked and their positions changed at least half-a-dozen times, and we more than once lost our way. I found the Zemski Natchalnik greatly perturbed. He had been buying hay for the peasants in the district, and the stock which had been delivered to him was half rotten. It was evident that he took a pride in the zealous discharge of his administrative functions, and a serious *contretemps* of this description caused him intense annoyance. He told me that his duties involved an immense amount of correspondence with the Government Department, to which he was responsible, and he spent the greater part of every day at his desk. The cares of office had made him nervous and irritable. He had received a liberal education, and had attained the position of a lecturer at his University when the office of Zemski Natchalnik was instituted. He then abandoned his scholastic career, and returned to his estate, in order to take up his present appointment. His ignorance of country life made his new post extremely difficult, but by dint of great application he has become an exemplary official.

Next morning I was present while he gave audience to the peasants, and I subsequently visited several of the surrounding villages. My host had erected a sort of dispensary, which was superintended by a German hospital nurse from Riga, a bright, energetic woman, who spoke Russian after a fashion, and was extremely popular among the peasantry. People came from far and near to consult her as to their ailments. Her remedies were of the most simple kind, and her theoretical knowledge was by no means profound; but her natural common sense and practical kindness were so great that the peasantry preferred her to the local doctors. The latter, for that reason, hated her cordially, and denounced her as a witch.

Saratoff has frequently been mentioned as one of the most distressed provinces, and I, therefore, came prepared to witness destitution of a heartrending description. What was my surprise to find in the villages I inspected a measure of comfort, decency, and cleanliness that compared most favourably with the squalor and misery that prevail in the other provinces I have traversed. The floors of the huts were clean, furniture of a certain sort adorned them, in some cases windows were even hung with curtains, while, in most instances, there were two rooms besides a living-room. This was the first rural district in which I had seen beds. Even the poorest peasants had bedsteads and bedding. The external appearance of the huts was also much neater. They were all made of well-trimmed logs, substantially put together, with good wooden roofs and handsome windows. The people seemed contented and happy. They did not complain that the relief the Zemstvo gave them was inadequate, but were all grateful, and expressed themselves satisfied. The Government allowed them fuel from the neighbouring forests. The Zemstvo distributed 36 lbs. of grain per head per month, and although this was not sufficient to last them through the month, it enabled them to tide over their difficulties, as they earned a little money by carting and other casual employment. In the autumn their condition was very precarious, but the Zemstvo had saved them.

I understand that this comparative comfort is due to the energy and influence of the late Governor of Saratoff, General Kossitch, who took up the question of providing for the peasantry in a thoroughly large-hearted spirit. In all the villages I visited I saw everywhere the same evidences of comfort and contentment. Much of this well-being is also due, no doubt, to the zeal of the Zemski Natchalnik and to the practical benevolence of his energetic sister, a young lady scarcely out of her teens, who has organised a branch of the Red-Cross Society, opened free dinners, and works night and day with a cheerfulness and hopefulness that are really touching. These two young people, Mr and Miss Schachmatoff, live by themselves in a long, white building, with windows resembling those of a church. It was formerly the school house, and is ill adapted for habitation, but it is warm, which their country house (intended only for residence during the summer) is not. They are orphans, and thus the entire burden of managing their estate, and looking after the peasantry, falls upon them alone. As the German hospital nurse wanted to go to Saratoff to purchase medicine and other dispensary requisites, I offered her a seat in my sledge, and very glad I was afterwards that she accepted. She knew the road perfectly, and directed the driver, who, but for her guidance, would certainly have lost his way again.

It was evening when we reached a village which stands half-way between Saratoff and the Zemski Natchalnik's estate. Here we proposed to drink tea in the Starosta's (elder's) hut, and we sent the driver to wake him up, but the slow, lumbering fellow was unable to make himself heard. We waited in the cold for about half-an-hour, and as neither driver nor Starosta appeared, I went myself to rouse the occupants of the hut. After falling several times in the snow, I reached a lighted window and knocked. There was no answer. I battered at the gate for some time, with no better result. Finally, I returned to the window, and knocked so violently in my impatience that I broke one of the panes. In a few seconds, I had a hornet's nest about my ears. Peasants came rushing out with axes to kill me. Women followed them, screaming and gesticulating. I was quite unarmed, so I shouted, "Don't make fools of yourselves, but let us in and give us tea." It took me a considerable time to explain that I had come from the Zemski Natchalnik, and was taking the celebrated nurse to Saratoff. At the name of the Zemski Natchalnik and the sight of the nurse, they were a little appeased, and at last we were admitted to the ample and many-roomed hut of the Starosta, and got tea. I now offered a rouble in payment for the broken window, but the peasants, who were by this time thoroughly ashamed of themselves, and frightened because I had threatened them with the terrors of the law, refused to take more than sixpence.

Close to the stove, huddled up in a corner of the hut, stood a curious little object, more like a wild beast than a human being. It turned out to be a German boy, from a German colony on the Samara side of the Volga, who was tramping his way to some other German colony in Saratoff, where he had relations. He told us that he had not had any food for days, and that the people in his village were all starving, and so he had started off to seek his relations in the province of Saratoff. He had no proper clothing, and in the terrible cold had suffered shocking privations. Both his cheeks, his nose and his hands were frost-bitten. Our phlegmatic driver told us that there were many in the condition of this wretched waif on the Samara side. "They have had a famine for the last fourteen years over there," he said.

Having drunk our tea and warmed ourselves, we resumed our journey towards Saratoff. We had been driving for an hour or two, when my companion said to me, "Do you see that village in the distance? That is the most ugly bit of road we have to travel. It is inhabited by thieves. They wrap themselves in white sheets at night, to look like the snow, and knock travellers on the head and rob them. So you had better keep a sharp lookout." As we got nearer to this peasant village, we met a long train of sledges, carrying loads into the country. The peasants who were driving them, instead of walking by the horses in the customary manner, kept behind their sledges to prevent the inhabitants of the village from pillaging them. We passed these peasants, and came nearer and nearer to the village of evil repute, the troika bell ringing out loud and clear in the frosty air, and announcing our arrival.

Suddenly there was the sound of a whistle in the distance. "Hark," said my companion, "that is their signal." I was now thoroughly on the alert, and regretted I had no revolver. The road was horribly rough, and it was as much as we could do to keep our seats. Presently we heard the whistle again. We were now driving through the village itself. "Drive! drive for your life!" screamed my companion; "here they are." Sure enough I could see distinctly, by the light of the stars, the figures of some five or six men running like demons past the huts which lined the broad roadway. It was an anxious moment. If they had overtaken us and stripped us of our furs we might have perished in the cold. Even our stolid driver was roused by the sense of danger, and lashed his horses till they seemed to fly. Just at this critical juncture we got into a ditch, and the sledge was almost overturned. We held on breathlessly, continuing to shout "Drive on!" to our Yamstchik. The sledge righted itself, and in another minute or two we had left our pursuers far behind.

These fellows are great cowards, and a good blow from the shoulder would probably have sent them flying, but I was so wrapped up in furs that I could scarcely move, and would have been at a serious disadvantage. The frost was so intense that in the few minutes during which I threw back my fur collar, and got my arms free for the impending emergency, my nose and the tip of my ear, besides the right forefinger, were frost-bitten. On my arrival at Saratoff I bought a revolver.

Travellers in this part of Russia must exercise great caution, especially when they have any considerable sum of money in their possession. Even the police are not to be trusted, as the following story will show. A year ago a foolish merchant went to a masked ball with 10,000 roubles in his pocket. He there struck up an acquaintance with two lieutenants of police, who were on duty. To these officers he confided the fact that he had a large sum of money with him, and he then proceeded to treat them and others present to champagne until he was thoroughly drunk. The lieutenants of police decided that he was not capable of going home by himself, and so they escorted him. On the way they robbed him of his money and decamped. There is justice, even in Russia. After a long and extremely edifying trial, which has just been concluded, these two police lieutenants have been cashiered, and have received long sentences of banishment to Siberia.

CHAPTER XI.

THE KOTZEBUÉ ESTATE.

My next expedition was a 300 mile drive down the banks of the Volga, which I undertook for the purpose of investigating the condition of the unfortunate German colonists, whose case is as hopeless as it well could be. Thanks to the good offices of Herr Sciffert, one of the wealthiest residents of Saratoff, and the Roman Catholic Bishop here, I was furnished with letters of introduction to the Protestant and Catholic clergy of the chief villages along the route I proposed to follow. My first halting place was Herr Sciffert's own estate — the largest, indeed, practically the only big estate in the district. It is about forty miles from

Saratoff, and is of interest to the student of Russia for several reasons.

In the eighteenth century this enormous estate of some 30,000 acres was granted by the Empress Catherine to the famous Kotzebué family, who planted a colony of "Little Russians" from their southern estates upon this uncultivated, uninhabited, but remarkably fertile tract of land. In those days the banks of the Volga were fringed with extensive forests, and the plough of the husbandman had to be preceded by the woodcutter's axe. Now, all this has been changed. The glorious forests of the Volga have disappeared — that river itself is growing shallow and insignificant in consequence—and the once fertile regions of Saratoff and Samara are rapidly becoming barren deserts, over which the hot winds of the summer sweep with devastating effect, burning up all vegetation in their path.

The celebrated estate of the once powerful Kotzebués is magnificent no longer, and has changed hands, part falling into the possession of a clever peasant, now a millionaire; the other and larger portion belonging to the descendant of a German colonist, Herr Seiffert.

The history of the Kotzebués and their estate is the history of the majority of the great Russian aristocratic houses. It is a record of wild and reckless extravagance, of bad management, neglect, and decay. The immediate cause of this general decline is the emancipation of the serfs, but the real cause lies deeper, and is at the root of the entire Russian system of government. Interesting as it is to find one of the former serfs of these great nobles now actually possessing the land which once belonged to the latter, it is hardly less curious to find transplanted a small colony of Little Russians, in a climate and in circumstances totally different from those of their original home. They have brought with them their customs and their national costume, their oxen and ploughs; their cottages are built on the South Russian plan, and their sunny southern faces have remained unaltered, notwithstanding the years and generations which have intervened since their migration. But their circumstances, recently at least, have grown truly desperate.

For something like three or four years there has been no harvest to speak of. The unfortunate peasants have sold their cattle and horses, and have literally nothing to eat except what the Zemstvo gives them. It is sad to find that the man from whom, more than any other, the peasants were entitled to expect sympathy and assistance—the estate owner, who has risen from their own ranks—does less for them than many nobles in other districts. He has opened no free dinners. He has established no regular system of relief. He and Herr Seiffert content themselves with giving occasional assistance to individuals as they present themselves. The 36 lbs. of corn which the Zemstvo gives every month, hardly suffices to keep the people alive. They are already becoming bloated and ill from the effects of bad food, and the appearance of the children especially is heartrending.

Many deaths have occurred, which would, in England, be set down to starvation; but the order has gone forth, that nobody shall die of starvation in Russia, this year at least, and so the doctors put the deaths down to paralysis of the heart and similar causes, when weakness, resulting from inanition, is the true one. Here I first saw inadequately clothed peasants, shivering in their fustian rags, children crying for food, and indescribable privation. But the cottages of the Little Russians are cleaner and neater than those of the Russians proper; and, notwithstanding the desperate straits to which these peasants have been put, they still retain their habits of neatness and cleanliness.

The tragic side of the situation is, that these peasants are involuntary colonists. They did not of their own free will seek out the shores of the Volga. They were brought there as serfs by their lord and master. It is doubtful, however, whether they are able to realise this particularly melancholy aspect of their fate. They are not intellectually advanced. The condition of their priesthood is deplorable. In the valley of Ruibushka, which has a population of 4000, the priest is an amiable and well-meaning man, who takes an interest in his parishioners, and manifests great sympathy with them in their suffering. Unfortunately, he is himself dependent upon the charity of the Zemstvo, and is unable to do anything to relieve the distress by which he is surrounded on every hand.

In one of the huts I entered I was so touched by the pitiable condition of the occupants that I gave them some money. At the sight of it the children absolutely wept for joy, knowing that they might hope to obtain at least one meal in the immediate future. In another hut I saw a fine, handsome young woman, by whose cheerful and pleasant manner I was much struck.

I asked her who she was, and was told that she was a cousin of the occupants, to whom she was upon a visit.

"Oh!" I said to the mistress of the hut— a wizened old woman, who seemed to be nothing but skin and bone—"then you are still able to be hospitable and entertain visitors."

At these heartless words, which I had only uttered in order to get a true insight into the condition of these poor people, the bright-faced young woman burst into a flood of tears, and then related to me, in her curious patois, Little Russian, her singularly chequered career. It throws an interesting light on that undiscovered country — the life of the Russian peasant. The young woman, after getting married, and working loyally for her husband in the hut and in the field, besides presenting him with several children, was suddenly left a widow. Now, according to Russian peasant custom, her life, never particularly rose-coloured, became sad indeed. Her own parents had got rid of her, and since she had married into another family and gone to another village, they had washed their hands of her. The parents of the late husband, now that the family had lost his share of the communal land, looked upon her and her children as drones whom they had to feed without getting any return. When, therefore, a suitor presented himself, the unfortunate woman was compelled to accept him and follow him to a distant village.

Soon afterwards, the famine broke out, and the peasant, a drunken fellow, began to thrash and starve his wife and children, and continually threatened to kill them. The village elder tried to establish peace and domestic happiness in the hut, but failed, and finally the poor woman was turned out by her brutal husband, the children were even stripped of their furs, and, almost naked, without food or money, they wandered back to the village from which they had been brought. But here no mercy awaited them. The parents of the unfortunate mother's first husband were anything but delighted to see her, and treated her quite as harshly as her second husband had done. She had sought refuge in the hut of another relative.

"What will you do next?" I asked.

The extraordinary helplessness and fatalism of the Russian peasant showed itself in her answer.

"God knows! Perhaps something will happen. I don't know, barin, what I shall do."

I was deeply touched by the spectacle of this unfortunate and absolutely helpless mortal. The priest, who accompanied me, assured me that there were hundreds and thousands of women in exactly the same plight as this young peasant.

"What is that?" he exclaimed. "It is the work of the *mir*, the village commune, with all the foulness which that barbarous system of land tenure entails. The village commune is popularly supposed to protect the peasant from pauperism. It would be more correct to say that it frequently artificially pauperises him, and it is certainly leading the entire Russian nation into abject misery."

One of the most grievous forms in which the tyranny of the village commune is felt at present is the system upon which are repaid the loans of bread and food, which the wealthier peasants make to the poorer ones, to enable the latter to tide over the days of starvation which set in at the end of the month, after the Government advances of flour have been consumed. These loans the poor peasant has to repay to his better-off neighbour as soon as he receives the following month's provisions, and prompt repayment is enforced by the community. Yet the Government relief leaves no margin for such repayment. The Starosta, or elder, is himself terrorised by the community, and forced to return on his list of destitute persons, not those whom he considers really necessitous, but those who insist upon being returned. Consequently, it frequently happens that the well-to-do and independent peasant receives aid, while the really poor are passed over.

The communal system is based upon joint responsibility for the taxes. Thus it is not the individual peasant who is taxed; it is the village community, consisting of so many "souls," or taxable units, and these are jointly responsible. The wealthy peasant may, therefore, have to pay the taxes of his poor and thriftless neighbour. This system is called the "*Krugovaya poruka.*" It has the effect of paralysing individual effort, but is supposed to be one of the fundamental institutions of "Slavonism," by which Russia is distinguished from Western Europe. How far the Krugovaya poruka is conducive to altruism the famine shows. Since the village commune is held responsible for the loans of corn from the Government, the rich, as well as the poor, desire a share of the corn advanced.

I was talking on this subject to a Zemstvo official here, when he replied,—"It is all very well for you to abuse the *mir*" (village commune), "but that form of land tenure seems to be particularly adapted to Russia. Take the German colonists, for instance. They arrived here with their German customs and institutions, and yet they found it expedient to adopt the Russian system of the village commune, and the *Krugovaya poruka*."

This speech was made before I had had an opportunity of visiting the German colonies. I have since learned that these settlers, truly enough, did find it expedient to adopt the Russian system of land tenure, because that was the condition upon which they were allowed to live in the country. But those most competent to judge, the colonists themselves, attribute the steadily increasing poverty and destitution from which they are suffering to this very system.

CHAPTER XII.

THE STORY OF THE GERMAN COLONISTS.

THE German colonists on the Volga number about 300,000. They may be roughly classified as Protestants, Catholics, and Mennonites. With the exception of the last mentioned, they all came over during the latter part of the 18th century, in response to a manifesto issued by the Empress Catherine. In that proclamation Catherine promised them certain privileges, the most notable of which were immunity from military service, self-government, and religious freedom. These privileges were granted "*na vek*," which means "for ever," but the "*vek*" of the Empress Catherine has recently been construed to signify a century only. There is just enough ambiguity about the expression to admit of this interpretation, but it is a quibble.

When universal military service on the German system was introduced into Russia, the German colonists were told they must either serve or go. Many of them, especially the Mennonites, who are a kind of Quakers, chose the latter alternative, and departed. The next thing to go was the self-government. The colonists used to be governed by a sort of elective council, which met at Saratoff, and was called the "Office." This body controlled the vagaries of the village commune. The "Office" has been abolished, and the Zemski Natchalnik now reigns in its stead. The German colonists have thus been gradually brought under the controlling influence of Russian institutions. Even their religion is threatened now. Fresh encroachments upon their civil and religious liberty are of almost daily occurrence, and their independence may already be described as a thing of the past. The steady decline in the fertility of the soil, which has culminated in chronic famine, and the inhospitable attitude of the Government, have brought home to the colonists that they have in Russia no abiding city. They are therefore emigrating in large numbers to the United States.

The advent of the Russian Zemski Natchalnik among these sturdy, honest Germans was quite uncalled for. The Zemski Natchalnik is a sort of substitute for feudalism. The Russian people are sadly in want of guidance and guardianship. As serfs they had their masters, who looked after them; but, since they have been emancipated, the village commune has led them a sorry dance. It is no part of the Tzar's policy to make the peasant an educated and independent member of society. Hence, it was found necessary, after twenty-five years of bad management and thriftlessness, to protect the peasant against himself, and put him under the tutelage of a Zemski Natchalnik.

Whenever possible, the people selected for this office were gentry resident in the neighbourhood, and already known and respected.

In the case of the German colonies there was, in the first place, no necessity to appoint such officers, and, in the second place, there were no gentry to select them from, consequently Government officials were appointed.

The authorities might have compromised the matter by selecting prominent colonists. There are not wanting among the German colonists men of energy and ability, who have, by dint of perseverance and industry, risen to wealth and influence. Thus the village of Messer, together with the whole of the surrounding neighbourhood, is practically dependent upon Herr Schmidt, originally a weaver by trade, who has become a miller and timber merchant as well, and is gradually monopolising all the trade of the district. But it did not suit the Government to appoint such men. The colonies were to be Russianised, hence Russian officials had to be appointed. The result was ludicrous in the extreme. These officials, with salaries ranging from £200 to £250 a year, arrived, armed with full powers, and commenced to give themselves airs. The influential colonists, however, passed the word among themselves, and the Zemski Natchalniki were boycotted. They could get neither lodging, nor food, nor any of the necessaries of life, so they had to capitulate and pay homage to the local magnate, who then, in nine cases out of ten, gave them free quarters, and thus was enabled to keep them in a proper state of humility and dependence.

The German colonists can only be described as so many nineteenth century Rip van Winkles. Imagine a body of men taken out of the eighteenth century, carefully preserved and kept apart from the influences of modern progress, latter-day customs and ideas, and you have the German colonists of the Volga. They all look like figures out of old German woodcuts, with their solemn, sallow, obstinate, cleanshaven faces, their hair dressed like a periwig, their gaunt forms, and their curious old-fashioned garments. They all wear stocks, and they are all very dignified and stately. They have still the same furniture which they brought with them more than a hundred years ago, and sleep in funereal four-post bedsteads. Their women, when young, have the pure and beautiful faces of the Gretchen type.

To come amongst these people in the midst of the semi-Oriental Russians is a great surprise to the traveller, and fills him with wonder. Their cottages are substantially built, and contain large and lofty rooms; yet the family generally sleep in one room, the heavily-curtained four-posters—of which I have seen as many as four in one room — securing almost as much privacy as so many separate apartments.

The condition of the colonists is really worse than that of the Russian peasants in other

The Story of the German Colonists. 165

districts, inasmuch as the former have no natural protectors or guardians. The estate owners to whom the Russian peasants formerly belonged, still take a sort of patriarchal interest in them, looking upon them as their own people, and helping them in their distress. But the German colonists have no one to whom they can look, except a few wealthy employers of labour. For hundreds of miles you can travel in the steppes which bound the Volga, without coming upon a country gentleman's seat. The colonists have a feeling that they are being left alone to die. No hand is stretched out to save them. Even the Government aid, scanty enough in all conscience, has been meted out more grudgingly and in smaller quantities to them than to others. The Red-Cross Society has passed them by altogether. This is how it comes about that, while the inhabitants of the Russian villages in Saratoff are fed, the Germans are starving. The moral the Russians point is different. They maintain that the existing state of things is an argument in favour of the Russianisation of the colonists.

As you enter a German colonial village you become aware of an extraordinary odour, heavy and unpleasant, which seems to pervade the whole neighbourhood. This is the odour of burnt manure, which the German colonist uses as fuel. In the beginning of the century, when Samara and Saratoff were virgin soil, an ingenious peasant invented a method of turning dung into bricks for fuel, and got a gold medal for his idea, instead of being hung for it. At present, the German colonist burns his manures, and puts nothing into the land, yet he wonders at its barrenness! It was touching, on entering the cottages, to see the industry of the inhabitants. All were busy, working for their very lives. Most of the colonists on what is called the mountainous side of the Volga are weavers, and by dint of very great labour they are able to earn about 6s. a month. This is not paid to them in cash, but in kind. They are all hopelessly in debt to their employers or sweaters, and these, of course, take full advantage of the circumstance. The only educated people amongst them are the clergy and the schoolmasters, and these have not received any salary for years. It is sad to see young children, with pale faces and glistening eyes, working at the looms like galley slaves. In one cottage that I entered, the owner, an old man of sixty-five, was lying in a semi-unconscious condition in his bed. He had not tasted food for several days, and his mind was wandering.

In some villages I saw men, women, and children sitting almost naked, unable to go out to seek work because they had no clothes, and excluded from the receipt of Government aid because they had a handicraft. This is, indeed, the worst feature in the administration of relief. The Government helps the absolutely destitute, whom it is scarcely worth while to save, and leaves those who are industrious and able-bodied to starve. In the Russian villages this arbitrary arrangement is tempered by the dishonesty of the *mir*, but the German colonists retain the sterling qualities which they brought with them from the Fatherland. They are sober, virtuous, honest, and industrious. Much of their present helplessness is due to the fact that they were originally handicraftsmen and tradesmen, and knew nothing about agriculture. They consequently adopted the methods common in Russia, and hence, instead of improving the Russians, they are gradually themselves sinking down to the same level.

Notwithstanding the honesty of the colonists on the Volga, crimes of violence are becoming common, and several clergymen informed me that burglarious attempts upon their own houses are of frequent occurrence. One Protestant clergyman told me that he had, only a few days before, found a corpse lying in the road, with marks of blood all round. No solution of the mystery had yet been discovered.

to them in cash, but in kind. They are all hopelessly in debt to their employers or sweaters, and these, of course, take full advantage of the circumstance. The only educated people amongst them are the clergy and the schoolmasters, and these have not received any salary for years. It is sad to see young children, with pale faces and glistening eyes, working at the looms like galley slaves. In one cottage that I entered, the owner, an old man of sixty-five, was lying in a semi-unconscious condition in his bed. He had not tasted food for several days, and his mind was wandering.

In some villages I saw men, women, and children sitting almost naked, unable to go out to seek work because they had no clothes, and excluded from the receipt of Government aid because they had a handicraft. This is, indeed, the worst feature in the administration of relief. The Government helps the absolutely destitute, whom it is scarcely worth while to save, and leaves those who are industrious and able-bodied to starve. In the Russian villages this arbitrary arrangement is tempered by the dishonesty of the *mir*, but the German colonists retain the sterling qualities which they brought with them from the Fatherland. They are sober, virtuous, honest, and industrious. Much of their present helplessness is due to the fact that they were originally handicraftsmen and tradesmen, and knew nothing about agriculture. They consequently adopted the methods common in Russia, and hence, instead of improving the Russians, they are gradually themselves sinking down to the same level.

Notwithstanding the honesty of the colonists on the Volga, crimes of violence are becoming common, and several clergymen informed me that burglarious attempts upon their own houses are of frequent occurrence. One Protestant clergyman told me that he had, only a few days before, found a corpse lying in the road, with marks of blood all round. No solution of the mystery had yet been discovered.

Another clergyman warned me solemnly against driving at night. I had just driven sixty miles in my sledge.

The Volga itself is a dangerous highway at night. Even the large caravans of merchandise which travel along its course are accompanied by escorts of armed men. The camel is a familiar beast of burden on the Volga and throughout Samara and Orenburg. It is very curious to see these graceful animals stepping daintily along through the snow, and drawing enormous loads. Will Samara become a Sahara? These camels suggest the comparison.

In the course of my drive down the Volga I had another unpleasant adventure. I was travelling alone, with only my coachman for company. As we drove along over the frozen river the ice under us made all sorts of mysterious noises. On our left were steep and barren rocks, on our right the open country, with bushes and underwood. A dull evening promised to turn into a dark night, and we had thirty miles still to cover before we got to the village which I hoped to reach. Suddenly we met, gliding along with a sort of cat-like agility, a strange individual in rags, with a musket of quaint construction slung over his shoulder, and a stout cudgel in his hand. He was walking towards us. As we passed he stood on one side, and humbly took off his cap. There was something about the fellow which did not please me, and so I looked round to see whether he had not climbed up behind, but he was continuing his journey.

We had driven about half an hour, and covered about four miles more, when my yamsthik got down to readjust the harness. All at once he turned round, and asked someone, apparently behind me, how far it was to the village we were bound for. I looked behind and saw the stealthy wayfarer with his gun. How he got there, I don't know. He must have run after the sledge and got up behind, with the intention of knocking me on the head as soon as we were within whistling distance of his comrades, for I had been told that the Volga was infested with bands of armed robbers, and half an hour later, when it had got quite dark, we heard ominous whistles from the bank, but fortunately met with no adventures.

The man with the gun looked at me hard, and I looked at him. He then carefully eyed the sleeve of my fur coat, and perhaps saw the end of my revolver peeping out, for he said, "God grant that you may arrive safely at your destination." He then left us. This time I kept a careful watch, to see that he did not climb up again, but I think he had understood my look. The famine has made the people desperate, and, though they are not of a blood-thirsty disposition, they will often murder for the sake of a few roubles.

On the Samara side of the Volga the condition of the people is worse and more helpless than on the Saratoff side. There they have no weaving, no industries of any kind, and are simply lying down to starve.

The following figures, which I obtained from a clergyman, show the condition of a typical village in Samara, and speak for themselves. The normal population of the village was 7856, but of this number, on the 1st of January last, 2765 were absent from various causes, while 78 were reported ill. At the corresponding period of 1886, the village was in a prosperous condition. All the people were well clad, had plenty of fuel, and possessed adequate supplies of bread and meat. There were also plenty of fodder for the cattle and horses. At the beginning of the present year, about one-third of the total number of families had absolutely no fuel, and an equal proportion had hardly any clothing, their only protection from the cold being a few miserable rags. Between the 1st of January 1886, and the 1st of January 1892, the number of horses had diminished from 3739 to 1667, the number of cows from

2385 to 602, and the number of sheep and goats from 6526 to 1962. At present some 1250 persons in this one village are dependent for their subsistence upon the relief they receive from the Zemstvo.

With regard to the prospects of next harvest, they are blacker than ever, as may be seen from the slender stock of grain that has been, and is available, for seed. The relative position in the village, as between the two periods compared, stood thus (a "dessiatine" being about $2\frac{3}{4}$ acres):—

	Jan. 1, 1886.	Jan. 1, 1892.
No. of dessiatines for which seed in hand..................	14,300	886
No. of dessiatines sown	3,850	1503

This means that some 15,761 dessiatines of grain-growing land, or, in English measurement, over 40,000 acres, must, in this single district of Samara, lie fallow in the present year for lack of seed. The calculation, if extended, even in a greatly modified form, to the famine-stricken districts generally, yield results which are positively appalling.

Since the month of September, the live stock of the village referred to above has been diminished by the loss of 611 horses, 162 oxen, 564 cows, 201 calves, and 2500 sheep and goats—in all, 4938 head of cattle. In addition to these losses, the indebtedness of the community has been increased during the past six years by 59,164 roubles. In 1886, it was 13,216 roubles; it now stands at 72,380 roubles.

Many of the colonists, to save fuel, have dug for themselves holes in the ground, and then constructed subterranean shelters, in which they burrow like foxes. In some of the villages they are eating bread made from wild hemp, and even the carcases of the horses that have died. I heard of a case in which a large number of people died from the effects of nausea produced by eating horse-flesh. There is a superstition among the the Germans, as well as the Russians, that the horse is an unclean animal, and not fit for food; hence the knowledge that they had eaten what they considered unclean food so worked upon the imaginations of the peasantry, that they were seized with nausea, and died.

The hardships, privations and subterranean life of these unhappy people are rapidly turning them into wild beasts. Only the other day a man hanged his daughter, a child of ten, by the neck, because she had not succeeded in getting him any food by begging. She was cut down in time, however, and recovered.

Another case was related to me of an old man, who came trembling to the clergyman's kitchen, and begged piteously for some bread for his little children. A loaf was given him, and at the sight of it his eyes glistened. He seized it wildly, tore it up ravenously, and commenced devouring it; then he suddenly remembered his starving children, uttered a piercing shriek; fell down in a fit, and died.

In Messer I was shown an old man of seventy-five, who had walked ten miles, carrying an enormous load of cotton which he and his family had woven. In repayment he received a bag of flour, weighing 36 lbs., and a few other necessaries, and with his fresh load he proceeded to walk back. His horses had been sold, and nobody would lend him one.

The Germans manage to get some nourishment out of a kind of tea made from the wild grass of the Steppes, and mixed with Spanish liquorice. In many of the villages this is all they have to live upon.

From further observations, I have come to the conclusion that the only way to rescue the German colonists from their present hopeless position is to assist them to emigrate. There are 300,000 of them. If 100,000 could be got over to Canada or the United States, the others would follow. All relief that may be administered to them here will only be palliative. The land is exhausted, the Volga is silting up, the climate is changing, and the only hope of salvation for this fine race of German colonists lies in their removal from this inhospitable country. If they remain, those who do not die of starvation will be gradually deprived of their religion, their language, and everything else that is distinctive of their race or of the land of their birth.

CHAPTER XIII.

NIJNI-NOVGOROD.

NIJNI-NOVGOROD is the principal bazaar town of Russia. During the summer months it is alive with a floating population of merchants and camp followers from every corner of this vast empire. The bazaar teems with Armenians, Bokharians, Persians, Jews, Tartars and Kirghis; Western Europe being represented by the hardy Scotsman and the frugal German. The noble Volga, swollen at this point to grand proportions by its tributary, the Oka, is gay with craft of every description. The bazaars are alive. The busy streets are thronged. Every conceivable object can be purchased, every variety of amusement obtained. Bands, cafés chantants and theatres vie with each other in affording entertainment to the enterprising merchant when his day's work is over. On the opposite bank rises the old town, with its gloomy fortress on the crest of a hill, the houses nestling closely round it. The sun glints upon the golden cupolas of the churches. All is life and animation. One feels that one is in a veritable human beehive.

A different spectacle meets the eye of the traveller in the winter. The endless streets of the bazaars are filled with snowdrift, and are desolate and deserted. An occasional watchdog, which snarls as you pass, is almost the only sign of life observable. The theatres and cafés look forlorn. No wayfarer meets you. The bazaars of Nijni are like a city of the dead. The Volga is a vast snowfield, in which the few frozen-up vessels look sadly out of place.

The old town on the hill is now the centre of life and business. Towards this town, the capital of a province as big as a European State, I hurried on through the dreary waste. Despite the desolation that surrounded me, I was impressed by the grandeur of the view. The only hotel in Nijni-Novgorod had been let out on the previous evening to a wedding-party, and was topsy-turvy. Part of it had been gutted by a fire a few weeks previously. The coffee-room was the Exchange, and all day long merchants and touts kept shouting, talking, and ringing little bells. I had been provided with a letter to the chief of the Statistical Bureau, and this gentleman placed the very ample material in his possession at my disposal. The figures that he gave me are quite as interesting, from a general point of view, as from that of the province of Nijni-Novgorod considered alone.

The famine has manifested itself in all the provinces it has visited in much the same manner. Everywhere I have found in the first place a large number of people, with every means of being well-informed, insisting on the absence of a famine. These gentlemen invariably tell you: "There is no famine in our province. Our peasants are well fed and contented. We have had a bad harvest, but we have no famine. If you want to see the famine you must go to the next province. There you will find real distress. The condition of the people there is indeed deplorable." On the other hand, there is a very large number of people, equally well informed, who tell you that there is no district so destitute as theirs, no suffering anywhere at all comparable to the sufferings of the peasants in their own particular neighbourhood.

The next feature, which helps to explain the callousness of one class, and the pessimism of the other, is the historical feature. All over Russia I have heard the following expressions:—"Our district is, agriculturally speaking, a squeezed-out lemon. The famine is not an isolated phenomenon, it is the climax of a series of bad years." This gradual decline in the fruitfulness of the soil has been accompanied by an increase of the population. The land at the disposal of the peasants has remained stationary, its fertility has diminished, and the number of mouths it has to feed has increased at an alarming rate. Hence the peasant has been in a chronic state of starvation for years, and his present distress is not so apparent to those who have been standing by and watching his decline, as it is to the new comer, or to the ardent reformer and intelligent patriot, who sees with aching heart the gradual ruin of his country. The peasant is the goose who lays Russia's golden eggs, and he is being slowly killed.

While the peasant is gradually growing poorer, the State is growing more and more exacting in the collection of taxes. The system adopted reminds one of the worst stories told against the French tax-farmers in the eighteenth century. In the province of Viatka, for instance, the governor determined to ignore the famine, and collect to the uttermost farthing the tribute due. He consequently despatched the vice-governor with the police officials, accompanied by soldiers and Cossacks, and several sledge loads of birch rods, on a tour of inspection in the villages. The simple method employed was to select the wealthiest peasants of a certain village, and flog them until the taxes were produced. In some cases the most merciless floggings failed to have the desired effect. There was literally no money to be got in these villages. The private property of the peasantry was sequestrated, their tea urns, their fur coats, their simple cotton clothing, their primitive agricultural implements — everything was seized. Then came the question of disposing of these goods and chattels. To collect them was an easier task than to sell them. Finally, Jews and exploiters of every kind presented themselves, and consented to purchase the various articles collected at so much a pood. The price per pood was the same whatever the article might be. Fur coats were sold for 6d. each. The most wanton spoiliation occurred. When the requisite sum had been realised, large numbers of articles remained. These the governor, in his wisdom, ordered to be redistributed to their owners, but they had been collected with such haste and violence, that no record had been kept of their proprietors. The governor's orders had to be carried out, however, and the most ridiculous confusion resulted. Widows received pairs of trousers; old men, the fur coats of children; bachelors cradles, etc.

I did not read this story in a Russian "Joe Miller;" it was told me by a solemn official, one of the wisest and most enlightened in his district, who implored me not to mention his name. "You know," he said, "the order of things in which we live. This is not a Government, but an Asiatic despotism. Perhaps if some of these, and similar facts find their way into the British press, they will make our rulers ashamed of themselves."

In this connection, a Russian lady once told me she blushed for herself and her country, that she and her compatriots should welcome with pleasure the journalists of Russia's hereditary enemies, and appear to make common cause with them. "It seems so unpatriotic and unnatural," she said; "but it is the only means we have of obtaining publicity for our grievances, and it is the kind of publicity which our Government dreads most."

The steady decline of the well-being of the Russian peasantry is significantly indicated by the following figures, which I have extracted from an official return of the Zemstvo of Nijni, showing the taxation of the province for the last ten years:—

Year.	Estimated Revenue. Rs.	Amount Collected. Rs.
1881,	3,335,118	3,203,165
1882,	3,377,676	3,069,051

Year.	Estimated Revenue. Rs.	Amount Collected. Rs.
1883,	3,634,550	3,069,996
1884,	3,241,123	2,730,708
1885,	3,094,607	2,736,166
1886,	2,603,915	2,297,821
1887,	2,461,398	2,527,859
1888,	2,487,401	2,505,896
1889,	2,484,742	2,138,376
1890,	2,483,059	1,609,718

In ten years, the estimated revenue from taxation had declined by 1,052,059 roubles, and the difference between the estimated revenue and the amount actually collected had risen from 131,953 roubles in 1881 to 273,341 roubles in 1890. In other words, while the estimated taxes had declined by a third, the arrears had doubled. The taxable power had declined, the insolvency had increased. It is the same in other provinces. *Pari passu* with this state of things, the expenditure of the country is increasing, and bankruptcy is staring Russia in the face. In another table, the total arrears of the province are given. These returns are even more striking :—

ACCUMULATED ARREARS.

	Roubles.
1881,	739,942
1883,	952,234
1884,	854,050
1885,	982,294
1886,	1,152,164
1887,	1,358,040
1888,	1,297,820
1889,	1,274,232
1890,	1,604,084
1891,	2,493,877

Such figures require no comment.

Cattle statistics for the province exist since 1864. In 1864, there were 1,241,145 head of cattle; in 1890, 855,802. To save space, it will be more convenient to show the gradual decrease in averages of nine years :—

1864-72.—Annual average, 1,115,092 head of cattle.
1873-81.—Annual average, 1,027,590 head of cattle.
1882-90.—Annual average, 993,862 head of cattle.

The population is increasing. If the number of head of cattle in the province had remained stationary, this would have marked a decline. As it is, the figures tell an appalling story of gradual impoverishment. In 1882, there were 261,421 horses in this province; in 1890, only 213,168. Of these, it is estimated that about 45 per. cent have been killed or sold during the winter of 1891-92. The remarks made above respecting the decline in cattle apply, of course, with even greater force to the stock of horses.

The province of Nijni-Novgorod has hitherto been regarded as one of the most prosperous in Russia. Its village industries were once famous. Nijni is the home of locksmiths, cutlers, leather-workers, turners, etc.; but all these industries have been on the decline for the last twenty years. Notwithstanding Nijni's favourable situation, notwithstanding the Volga and the annual fair, modern industrial methods are rapidly supplanting the old ones. Capitalists erect factories, with which the handicapped peasants cannot compete; and the railways bring the goods produced in Poland, Tula and Moscow within reach of the poorest purchaser.

CHAPTER XIV.

THE PEASANTS OF NIJNI.

In the last chapter I have illustrated, by official statistics, the deplorable economical condition of the province of Nijni. I will now give an account of my own personal observations among the peasantry in the villages I have visited. This can best be done by taking one or two typical instances. Here is a hut without flooring; as you enter it you tread upon the bare ground. There is no fuel for the big stove, and the hut is inadequately warmed by a small charcoal brazier placed in the centre. The occupants have sold their sheepskins. Their monthly allowance of bread lasts them for two weeks and a half. Three families have sought refuge in this single hut, and burn alternately their respective stores of fuel, consisting almost exclusively of the roofs of the two deserted huts, and even the woodwork of the huts themselves. Being without sheepskins these famishing peasants are unable to seek work, to go begging, or to do anything but to sit passively huddled together bemoaning their wretchedness.

Cases of suicide are common. Here is a typical example. A solitary peasant, without relations or friends, landless and helpless, had earned his living honestly for years as a shepherd. He was 55. The famine overtook his village, and he lost his occupation. The villagers had no food for themselves, still less for him. What was he to do? Despair seized him, and he put an end to his joyless life. In another case which was brought to my knowledge, the father of a family committed suicide in the following circumstances. He was 39, and had failed to obtain work. After starving for a fortnight the hopelessness of his case and the cries of his hungry little ones were too much for him. He begged from house to house for three days, and collected a few crusts and a little flour, which he did not touch himself, but gave to his children. He then relinquished the struggle, and died by his own hand.

The custom of giving alms "in the name of Christ," which is universal in Russia, and is one of the most beautiful traits in the character of the people, has not proved of much avail to the destitute this winter. Where all are in want, who is to help? There are two forms of alms-giving in Russia. One is the form referred to above. Mendicants knock at the doors and windows of dwellings, bow to the ground, and mutter, "for Christ's sake."

The peasant housewife instantly collects a few crusts and gives them to the applicant. It is considered a sin to turn the petitioner away, and even in such large towns as Moscow and St Petersburg this practice is kept up.

The stranger is forcibly reminded of it every time he enters a Russian baker's shop, and sees how the stale bread is kept in a kind of bin, and freely given to those who beg for it "in the name of Christ."

There is yet another custom which is still more touching. It is called the practice of "secret charity." A family is known to be in want, but is too proud to beg. Then the neighbours determine to help it without offending the feelings of its members. After sundown a tap is heard at the destitute family's window, and the simple words "for Christ's sake," are borne in to them. The peasant runs out to see who is there, but he finds no one. No trace of a visitor is left except a few footprints in the snow, and a piece of bread on the window ledge.

People with such customs must have been long inured to hardship and privation, but this year the bow has snapped. The old usages of orthodox Russia have failed to keep want

from the door. There has been no one to practise them. The following is an extract from an official report to the *Nijni Zemstvo* :—
"Many of the peasants in this district have reaped nothing but tares. Potatoes have been very bad. There is absolutely not food for the winter. The peasants have, besides, no forests of their own, and the Government forests are far off; the famished horses are too weak to carry the wood from such a distance, and consequently the peasants have to purchase their fuel for heavy prices from the local gentry, and there is no money anywhere." These few official words bear witness to the hopelessness of the situation.

It is pitiful to find the country gentry, the former proprietors of these destitute peasants, playing the part of usurers, and taking advantage of the people's necessities to get them into their power. The Jews are being turned out of the country, but the worst possible kind of usury is still practised.

The attitude of the gentry towards the distressed peasants is in many cases most inhuman. The peasant is regarded simply as motive power, as an agricultural implement. When he goes to the gentleman for assistance, the latter helps him on the following condition, that he is to work his, the gentleman's fields, before his own, and for nothing. M. Potapenko, a young novelist of great power and promise, has drawn some admirable pictures of the working of this system. The peasant often risks losing his own crops—being completely ruined, in fact—while he is harvesting for the gentleman. The weather changes, rain comes on; and while the gentleman's crops are safely stacked and housed, the peasant's are beaten down, and destroyed by the pitiless storm. The peasants are free only in name; their present bondage is more grievous to bear than that of thirty years ago, when it was at least their masters' interest to keep them well-fed, and in good condition.

In many parts of Novgorod, the peasants are living on mushrooms and bread made from tares and husks. The gentry have been slow in recognising the famine, and for that reason the Zemstvo has not been able to distribute relief as early as it ought to have done. Anxious to improve their condition, and help themselves, the peasants of Nijni, who are amongst the most intelligent in Russia, early prepared to face the famine. Many of them sold all they had, and emigrated to Siberia and other provinces, but their wanderings seldom brought them to a land of promise, and, in many instances, they were ordered back to their native districts by the police.

The emigration problem in Russia is a burning question. On the one hand, the most fertile districts of central Russia are exhausted, and in the "squeezed-out lemon" condition; on the other hand, there are vast districts of fertile soil in Siberia only waiting to be "tickled with a harrow to laugh with a harvest." Notwithstanding the rapid increase of the population, nothing is done to organise emigration. In fact, every obstacle is thrown in the way; and even when, after much trouble, the unfortunate peasants succeed in getting as far as Tiumen, they are generally left to starve. The Government does nothing to find them land or settlements, and the unfortunate exiles wander about like sheep without a shepherd, and generally return to their native villages poorer and sadder, if not wiser, than when they left.

This is the kind of thing that happens. I quote from a Reuter telegram which appeared the other day in the papers:—

"Fourteen thousand emigrants, who left Russia in consequence of the famine, have arrived at the Siberian town of Tiumen, on the road to Tobolsk, in a most miserable condition. Having exhausted all their resources on the journey, they are now in want both of food and clothing. They are, moreover suffering from diseases of all kinds; and their condition is hopeless, as their want of means prevents them from either continuing their journey or returning to their homes. Many have already died, either from disease or the frightful privations they have undergone."

The reason of this shameful neglect is twofold. In the first place, I am convinced, from what I have seen in the course of my journey through the country, that it is the deliberate policy of the Government to keep the peasant in a state of barbarism and poverty. Anything like culture or improvement is dreaded, for fear of awakening ideas that might be antagonistic to the autocracy. Where the Government stops short, the country gentleman steps in. It is his aim and object to keep the peasantry in a state of dependence, and to keep the wages of agricultural labour at the lowest possible level. The policy of the country gentry, in fact, reminds one forcibly of the man who tried to see how little he could feed his horse on. As in the case of that ill-starred quadruped, the Russian peasant has now been practically reduced to the starvation point.

Many of the peasants who were too cautious to emigrate, sought work in the towns and neighbouring villages, but their endeavours were fruitless; they had to return without work and penniless, to bear the reproaches of their starving families. There was no work to be found during these hard times. Even in the best of times it would have been difficult to find employment for the enormous numbers that went out to seek it. In a single district of this province, where the average annual exodus of factory hands and other labourers is about 5000, as many as 14,500 persons left the country in search of work. From these figures, some idea may be formed of the extent to which the labour market has been flooded.

A large proportion of the peasants who came

to the local authorities for travelling passports were unable to return to their homes. They were so weak and faint that the district passport clerks had to feed them to enable them to start. Many stated they had eaten only once in two days, some only once in three, and others but once in four days. The doctor of the fifth section of the Vassilski district, Dr Gerchen, reported that peasants presented themselves to him looking like living skeletons. In many villages the peasantry supported life on dried leaves, on tares, and on weeds. The case has been to a considerable extent met by the action of the Zemstvos in distributing corn, but the relief has been hopelessly inadequate.

The Zemstvo also supplied the peasantry with seed to sow their fields, but in many cases the peasants kept the seed for food and neglected to sow their fields. The prospects for next year's harvest are exceedingly good in Nijni-Novgorod, and, indeed, all over the Northern and Eastern provinces, for in these districts there has been a bountiful fall of snow. In the central provinces, however, there has been scarcely any snowfall at all during the winter, and things look very bad. Under normal conditions the prospects for Nijni-Novgorod would be considered excellent, but they must be discounted by the following considerations :—In the first place, by the great diminution in the stock of cattle and horses, and, in the second, by the diminution of the area under cultivation. The official statistics for the nine districts of Nijni-Novgorod which have suffered most give the following percentages of unsown fields, and it is safe to assume that they represent optimistic rather than pessimistic estimates :—

District.	Percent. of unsown peasant land.
Ardatoffski	24·8
Lukoyanoffski	15·5
Gorbatoffski	14·6
Arzamasski	11·8
Makaryeffski	6·3
Nijigorodski	4·1

District.	Percent. of unsown peasant land.
Knyagininski	3·8
Vassilski	2·2
Sergatski	1·6

To say that bankruptcy is staring the province of Nijni-Novgorod in the face is to make a statement of one province which is equally true of all the famine-stricken districts. In the other provinces I was not able to obtain such detailed statistics. Yet, notwithstanding these figures, appalling and eloquent as they are, there are earnest and perfectly honest officials in Nijni who have helped to compile these very statistics, and have travelled through the worst districts, and yet maintain that Nijni is comparatively prosperous, and has not been touched by the famine to the same extent as other provinces.

The terrible thing about this belief is that it is true. In Samara, Riasan, Pensa, Simbirsk and Kazan the situation is actually much worse and even more hopeless. Competent authorities have told me that it will take Russia ten years to recover from the effects of the famine. In Nijni, fortunately for the population, there is an energetic and liberal governor, General Baranoff, who has done all in his power to aid the peasants in their fight with the demon of hunger. He promptly prohibited the export of all bread stuffs from his province. By that measure he excited great discontent among the corn merchants, but its result was to reduce prices to something like a normal level; and he has also done much to encourage private charity and to help the peasants.

CHAPTER XV.

A DRIVE TO KAZAN.

THE journey from Nijni-Novgorod to Kazan in winter is arduous and unpleasant. In summer the trip down the Volga is most enjoyable, but a drive over the same river in the dead of winter, with a cold wind in your teeth all the way, is a very different matter. It seems strange that so important a town as Kazan, with its 140,000 inhabitants, its university, and numerous industries, should be cut off from all communication with the outer world during seven months in the year; but so it practically is. It takes forty-eight hours' hard travelling to cover the three hundred miles that separate Nijni-Novgorod from Kazan. One would imagine that, the railway from Moscow to Nijni having been once made, it would not have taken long to continue the line to Kazan. But Russia is a peculiar country.

Kazan has been agitating for a railway for a long time, and at last the scheme for the so-called Moscow-Kazan railway has been sanctioned and guaranteed by the Government. But this line is not to run from Nijni. That would be opposed to the great Russian principle of never carrying a railway parallel with a river. The line will, therefore, be run from Riasan, a very much greater distance. The peculiar feature of the scheme is, that the railway will not run to Kazan at all, but will stop short thirty miles from that city, at a certain point on the Volga, from which it will be continued to Perm, in order to tap the great iron districts of the Ural. The consequence is that the very city for whose benefit the railway is being built will not only be left out in the cold, but will be practically ruined.

It is said that this crazy scheme is due to the desire of certain officials holding a high position in the financial world to send up the price of the company's shares for their own immediate profit.

The sledge in which I accomplished the journey to Kazan was one of the most curious vehicles I ever saw. It was made of basket-work, painted green, and was surmounted by an enormous hood of the same colour. It was long, broad, and clumsy, and it possessed no seat or cushions, but it was lined throughout with felt. The bottom was covered with hay. Into this remarkable vehicle I threw myself, a helpless bundle of furs and rugs. The driver crossed himself, the waiters and porters of the hotel and a crowd of beggars called upon the Almighty to bless my journey, the horses' bells jingled, and off we went, every inequality of the road duly registering itself upon my back by bumping it. At distances averaging from ten to twenty miles we changed horses, and at each stoppage I got out to warm myself in the post-houses, which were all very dirty, and occasionally to drink a cup of tea and to eat a slice of sausage. I had to take my own provisions with me, and these got rapidly frozen. Several times between the posting stations the horses fell down and refused to get up again. There was then nothing for it but to go in search of fresh relays, which we generally procured at the nearest village. The wretched animals were little more than skin and bone. Their backs were covered with raw sores, which the irritation of the harness frequently caused to bleed. Along the road were scattered numerous carcasses and skeletons of horses which had died in harness.

The appearance of the post-houses was so uninviting that I determined to travel for forty-eight hours without a break, and to spend the two nights driving, so as to get the journey over as rapidly as possible. It was a beautiful sight to see the sun rise over the vast fields of snow, painting them almost purple. The ordinary colours do not obtain; light is pink, shadow blue, on the snowfields of the Volga. Facing the river-side villages were large crosses, skilfully cut out of blocks of ice, and most carefullly finished, some of them being 12 feet and 15 feet high. They had been erected for the ceremony of blessing the river. In some cases regular shrines, with handsome pillars and altars, all of clear blue ice, had been most beautifully carved. The Russian peasant does all his work with his axe. Here and there vessels were being built for the spring, and occasionally one came across a paddle-wheel, or even saloon-deck steamer frozen up, looking quaint and out of place.

Soon we got into the districts of the Tcheremissi, a Finnish tribe, and the aboriginal inhabitants of the northern part of Kazan. These people look picturesque in their caftans of coarse white cloth, which contrasted well with their dark olive complexions, their black moustaches, and Chinese eyes. I saw very few beards. This tribe is the most frugal, sober, and hard-working of the many people that inhabit the Tzar's dominions, and yet they have suffered terribly by the famine. Nowhere did I see such pitiful children as in the villages of Tcheremissi. They had the peculiar pallor and sharpness of feature which we usually associate with hunger. I distributed small coins amongst these poor little mortals, and it was touching to see them run off to their parents' huts with the money and then return to thank me. The women are pretty and of the Madonna type.

Dr Smirnoff, Professor of Ethnography at the University of Kazan, gave me the following interesting facts about the population of this vast province:—The aboriginal inhabitants, as far as is known, of the northern and western districts of Kazan were Finnish tribes, the

Tcheremissi inhabiting the west, the Mordvins and Votyaks the north. The southern and eastern districts were inhabited by the ancient Bulgars, from whom are descended the present Tchuvashi. These aboriginal tribes still remain, though they are fast dying out. They are nominally Christians of the Orthodox Church, but many are still heathens, and worship in groves. I have a very interesting account of the religious rites and prayers of the Tcheremissi, which was given me by M. Netchayeff-Maltzeff, a *maréchal* of the Imperial Court, and the Kazan Commissioner of the Heir Apparent's Committee, to whom I am indebted for much kindness and information. The following simple prayer is probably repeated with especial fervour during this year of trial:—

" God, great and good, send Thy heavenly mists down upon us, draw the mists of the earth to Thee! God, great and good, in the midst of the two mists cause the seed we have sown to grow fruitfully. Send us gentle breezes.

contrasted well with their dark olive complexions, their black moustaches, and Chinese eyes. I saw very few beards. This tribe is the most frugal, sober, and hard-working of the many people that inhabit the Tzar's dominions, and yet they have suffered terribly by the famine. Nowhere did I see such pitiful children as in the villages of Tcheremissi. They had the peculiar pallor and sharpness of feature which we usually associate with hunger. I distributed small coins amongst these poor little mortals, and it was touching to see them run off to their parents' huts with the money and then return to thank me. The women are pretty and of the Madonna type.

Dr Smirnoff, Professor of Ethnography at the University of Kazan, gave me the following interesting facts about the population of this vast province :—The aboriginal inhabitants, as far as is known, of the northern and western districts of Kazan were Finnish tribes, the

Tcheremissi inhabiting the west, the Mordvins and Votyaks the north. The southern and eastern districts were inhabited by the ancient Bulgars, from whom are descended the present Tchuvashi. These aboriginal tribes still remain, though they are fast dying out. They are nominally Christians of the Orthodox Church, but many are still heathens, and worship in groves. I have a very interesting account of the religious rites and prayers of the Tcheremissi, which was given me by M. Netchayeff-Maltzeff, a *maréchal* of the Imperial Court, and the Kazan Commissioner of the Heir Apparent's Committee, to whom I am indebted for much kindness and information. The following simple prayer is probably repeated with especial fervour during this year of trial :—

"God, great and good, send Thy heavenly mists down upon us, draw the mists of the earth to Thee! God, great and good, in the midst of the two mists cause the seed we have sown to grow fruitfully. Send us gentle breezes.

Give us peace! Let the three kinds of cattle multiply, make them fruitful, give them peace and health! Prosper our families, and give them peace! Preserve us from fire and water. God, great and good, as the sun shines, as the moon rises, as the sea is full, so prosper the seed we have sown, so prosper our families, increase our cattle, increase the silver of the treasury; with every prosperity, God, great and good, gladden and bless us."

Besides these aboriginal inhabitants, the province of Kazan has a large Tartar population. In the thirteenth century, Kazan was conquered by the Tartars, who made the town their capital. In 1552 the Russian conquest of Kazan took place. There are still numerous country gentlemen in Kazan, Penza, and even Tamboff, descended from Tartar princes. These, of course, have all become Christians, for in the seventeenth century, when the peasants were made serfs, the Christian peasants on the estates of Mussulman gentry were exempt from the new law, unless the Mussulmans embraced the Orthodox religion, which, of course, a great many did. Those who remained true to their religion have sunk to the level of the common peasant. In Kazan itself there is still a Tartar town, and among the ornaments of Kazan society are a Tartar general and his wife, both Mussulmans.

At one of the post-houses, I met a very intelligent postmaster, with whom I discussed the condition of the people.

"Perhaps you have heard, sir," he said, "that the peasants have refused to work, and will not execute the public works which the Government has undertaken, in order to relieve the famine-stricken districts. Of course, people who do not understand the question, maintain that there can be no famine and no privation since the lazy peasants won't work. But how can you expect them to work at the wages offered, and with the food and fodder as high as it is? To work for these wages would mean absolute ruin to the peasant, starvation for his horse, and, eventually, starvation for himself. Why should he work and sweat, in order to become even worse off than he is? If he must starve, it is easier for him to lie down peacefully and do so, than to work into the bargain. Our officials in St Petersburg do not know anything about the peasant and his circumstances, and do not even give themselves the trouble to learn; that is why so many mistakes are made. General Annenkoff is coming down here, and is going to have sleepers and telegraph poles cut, and all sorts of nonsense, at wages which mean starvation. Of course the peasants will refuse to work for those wages, and then they will be solemnly accused of laziness by the wiseacres at St Petersburg."

I felt that there was a great deal of truth in this tirade, and that it threw a new and interesting light on the question of famine relief works. It seems a violation of the laws of political economy, that in times of famine the market value of labour should be higher than in good years. But when we remember that money is only a counter representing food, we shall not be surprised to find that wages cannot fall below starvation limit.

It was curious to come across the bivouacks of caravan drivers, resting for the night, and sleeping round blazing fires in the snow. The caravans themselves were interesting. Every conceivable article of merchandise is carried between Nijni and Kazan, from Government stores of gunpowder to pianos.

At last, in the grey and misty dawn, we reached Admiraliteyskaya Sloboda, the suburb of Kazan. We dashed down the steep bank of one side of the Volga, and flew across the ice, to scramble up an almost perpendicular ascent on the opposite bank. The Admiraliteyskaya Sloboda is about three miles from Kazan, which, like many of the ports of the Volga, is not on that river at all. Kazan looks handsome as one approaches it. It is built upon a hill, on the crest of which rises the kremlin, or fortress. The entire town is white, the houses being all plastered, and the roofs a dark green. This, in the white snow, with nothing to relieve the monotonous effect but the cupolas of the churches, is wearisome to the eye. At the foot of the Russian city lies the Tartar town, with its tall minarets and quaint buildings.

The hotel that had been recommended to me happened by good fortune to be the one at which were staying most of the officials from St Petersburg sent to inquire into the famine. I took an early opportunity of calling upon M. Netchayeff-Maltzeff, to whom I have already referred, and was received by that gentleman with unexpected cordiality. "I have read your articles about the Russian famine in the English papers," he said. 'From your description I gather that you have been near my estate. All I can say, is that your accounts are perfectly accurate and truthful. It was pleasant to read such perfectly unbiassed statements."

M. Netchayeff-Maltzeff then went on to give me some very interesting information, but this I must reserve for my next chapter.

CHAPTER XVI.

THE TARTARS.

I MENTIONED in my last chapter that I had made the acquaintance of M. Netchayeff-Maltzeff, the Kazan Commissioner of the Famine Relief Committee, of which the Cesarewitch is president, and that he had given me some very interesting information concerning the condition of this province. I will endeavour to reproduce, as nearly as possible, in his own words what he told me :—

"The province of Kazan," he said, "has a population of 2,100,000. Of this total, about 300,000 represent the urban population, leaving 1,800,000 for the rural districts, of whom the Zemstvo is feeding about 800,000, and my committee 400,000. There are, besides, numerous private charitable organisations. The Baroness Uxkuell von Hildebrandt, for instance, is travelling about the country, organising free dinners, and her example has been followed by many others. We have had much trouble in getting at the truth of things here. The peasantry, especially the Tartars, are a lazy lot, and are only too glad to avail themselves of eleemosynary aid. I have adopted the following plan. In sending the members of my commission about the country, I have always sent a doctor with them. The doctor is able to certify whether the people are really starving. In some cases, my commissioners found the peasants lying down, declaring themselves too weak to rise. But the doctors generally found that their pulses were normal, and their condition by no means so desperate as they pretended. Nevertheless, there is a great deal of suffering and privation amongst them. There was absolutely no rain last year, and hence the harvest has been frightfully bad. Kazan had only 18 per cent. of a good harvest. Practically, the entire population is in a state of pauperism. Some of the villages are snowed up, the peasants have eaten their horses, and there is no getting in or out. There are villages completely cut off from all communication, and we cannot tell what is going on there.

"The Tartar population presents the most serious difficulties. There fatalism is the great obstacle to any attempt to stir them to activity. When they have money, they spend it on dress and pretty trinkets, and leave the future to take care of itself. They are also very bad agriculturists, but born pedlars. A Tartar will not mind hawking oranges about all day, but he will object to doing a few hours' honest work. The fatalism of the Tartars makes them appear uncharitable. I have had the greatest difficulty in moving the wealthy Tartars of the town to contribute towards the relief of their own people. They look upon the famine as a visitation of Providence, and consider it impious to try to thwart the will of Allah. Nevertheless, I have succeeded in getting the Tartar merchants of Kazan to open a free dinner-table, and at this Christians and Tartars are fed alike. Meat is the staple food. The Tartars receive horseflesh; the Christians, who will not eat it, get other meat. Altogether, the town of Kazan feeds daily at free public dinner table as many as 5000 people. The question that is giving me most uneasiness at present is the supply of horses. The Tartars have eaten theirs, and the horses of the other peasantry have mostly been killed for their hides. We are going to open refuges for those that remain, where we will feed them gratis, on one condition, only—namely, that every peasant whose horses we have fed shall undertake to plough a certain proportion of the village land besides his own share. The Government are going to grant 10,000 horses to the province, but that will be very little.

"I suppose you know that we are in the home of village industries. The chairs and tables in this room have all been made by the peasants of Kazan. Do you know that the entire carriage trade of Russia, Siberia, Central Asia, and even Persia, is in the hands of Kazan peasants? The peasants of Kazan make the heavy sledges, called tarantasses, for the Siberian roads. They also make the light carriages which one finds in Bokhara and Samarcand. The fashionable world of St Petersburg and Moscow drive about in vehicles made by Kazan peasants. Consequently, in ordinary years, the peasant in this province is well off. He has many industries to employ him in the winter. But the famine is felt in every branch of trade and industry, and the peasants have neither corn to sell nor orders to execute. The village industries of Russia are a very interesting study. It would be well worth your while to travel up the Kama, for instance, to Perm, and see the enormous sea-going vessels that are built there. The steamers of the Caspian and the Black Sea are built on the Kama. Every kind of iron industry flourishes there; even locomotives and steam engines are built at Perm, and sent down to the south."

M. Netchayeff-Maltzeff gave me a most vivid picture of the trade and life of the Volga, that sadly neglected artery of Russian commerce. M. Netchayeff-Maltzeff had been sent to inspect Kazan because the Governor had refused to admit that such a thing as famine could occur in his province. The Minister of the Interior had sent to accompany M. Netchayeff-Maltzeff an official from his department, and there were, besides, two young gentlemen and two doctors attached to the mission. M. Netchayeff-Maltzeff signalised his advent by giving 25,000 roubles out of his private means towards the relief of the distressed.

Kazan was full of commissions when I arrived, and in a state of some excitement. There was, among others, a commission to investigate the distribution of the Zemstvo relief, for serious malpractices had been brought to light in connection with the local administration. A young merchant of Kazan, who had organised a relief committee of his own, discovered, amongst the flour distributed by the Zemstvo, bags of pulverised reeds, and similar adulterations. These discoveries led to the summary dissolution of the committee in question, as it was looked upon with suspicion for ferreting out such abuses, but they also led to the appointment of a Government commission of inquiry.

An epidemic of typhoid fever was raging. Peasants were being brought in in cart-loads. The hospitals were full. In all directions the most horrible sights met the eye. Young women were brought into the town in a state of perfect nudity, except for some scraps of matting that were thrown over them in the cart. The destitution of the people is something terrible, and the streets are filled with beggars.

Considerable excitement was caused recently

by the trial of a young man for an attempt to murder the Governor. This youth had heard stories of the terrible privation and suffering which existed, and knew that the Governor had refused to acknowedge the existence of a famine. In order, as he declared, to attract public attention to the state of affairs, this young fanatic went into the audience chamber of the Governor to present a petition. As the Governor held out his hand to take the document, the young man fired a revolver at him without doing him any injury, and without intending to do him any, as he avers. The prisoner has been sentenced to penal servitude in the mines of Siberia, but has appealed. The case is being hushed up as much as possible, but the supposed attempt on the Governor's life served its purpose, and the famine in Kazan was officially acknowledged.

The history of the Governor's attitude in regard to the famine is worth relating. The Government instructed M. Vishnyakoff, an official of the Ministry of the Interior, to report upon the famine in Kazan on his way back from Saratoff and Samara. He remained twenty-four hours in Kazan, and reported that there was no famine. The Governor was then instructed to make a personal tour of inspection. He ordered the Chief of Police, the Ispravnik of the district, to make arrangements. The Ispravnik purchased a number of cakes and buns, and had them distributed among certain villages. He then took the Governor round these villages, and into the huts where the buns had been distributed, and satisfied the Governor that there could be no famine, since the peasants were actually eating buns and cakes.

Subsequently the attitude of the Government changed. The reports in the press were too alarming, and too well substantiated to be ignored. Philemonoff, a village priest, sent a letter to the *Moscow Viedomosti*, in which he stated that he had administered the Eucharist to, at least, twenty peasants who had died from starvation. There was an unaccountable delay in the publication of this letter, but, when it appeared, it raised a storm, and the Government were forced to recognise the famine. Consequently, the Governor of Kazan, M. Poltaratski, received the requisite instructions. He now developed an extraordinary kind of activity. He collected donations from the wealthy merchants of Kazan, and then proceeded on a tour round his province, accompanied by the same Ispravnik who had helped him on the previous occasion.

This time there was to be no mistake about it. There was to be a genuine famine, and consequently, as the Governor drove into the village, he found the roads lined with peasants, who implored his help, calling him their benefactor and food-giver. The Governor distributed amongst them the money he had collected and drove on. Of course his method of relieving the distress did no permanent good. It had only one result. It effectually closed the pockets of the charitably inclined, who refused to trust their donations to the Governor. Even the rich merchants of Moscow, who had sent large quantities of corn to Kazan, would not allow him to distribute it. They sent an agent of their own into the villages to aid the necessitous. But an over-zealous Zemski Natchalnik sent his agent a note, in which he informed him, that unless he left the neighbourhood immediately he would have him turned out by the police. The agent rushed off to Kazan, and petitioned the Govenor for permission to relieve the distressed. By this time things had changed considerably in Kazan; M. Netchayeff Maltzeff had arrived, and a new attitude had been taken; consequently the clerk received a permit to travel over the province and go where he liked.

In view of this incident, and upon the advice of several gentlemen to whom I had letters of introduction, I waited on the Governor, and told him I had come to ask permission to travel over his province.

"Go, in God's name," he said, "I can't pervent you. I have no right to do so," he added, mournfully. "But I will do all I can for you. My Ispravnik shall take you about, and show you all you want to see."

I confess I had not foreseen the possibility of such a turn of events. This was the very Ispravnik who had distributed the buns. That evening an officer in uniform, with a long white moustache, called on me. He was the Ispravnik. Next day I returned his visit.

'I asked his Excellency," he said, "whether you spoke Russian, and his Excellency replied, 'Better than we do.' That made me anxious to meet you," he continued, "because I wondered whether you were not an emigrant" ("emigrant" being a euphemism for an escaped convict or Nihilist). "I thought you might be a friend of mine whom I knew many years ago," and he mentioned the name of a prominent Nihilist who lives in London. Needless to say that I felt uncomfortable, and directly determined to give the affable Ispravnik the slip. He was very chatty, and even read to me his confidential report to the Governor upon the famine, which might have been written by Count Tolstoi himself, so extremely liberal was it in tone. He pointed out the mistake of assisting only the very destitute, and the importance of supporting the comparatively well-to-do families as well.

The Ispravnik is an official of great importance. There is one to every district, and he is the police officer, the tax-collector, and represents generally the Executive, while the Zemski Natchalniki, of whom there is a considerable number in a district, represent the Administration. The province of Kazan has an area of 56,000 square versts. The district of the same name has an area of 5000 square versts, and contains 49 settlements—that is, towns and villages; and these the Ispravnik has to keep in hand. He told me his people gave him little trouble, and, with the exception of an occasional riot amongst the Tartars, things worked very smoothly.

"The Tartars drink fearfully," he said; "they are all drunkards, they and their mullahs (priests) together. You know our system of tax-collecting, of course? The Ispravnik, who collects the full amount of taxes due, gets £30 as. a gratuity. I am thankful to say, that I have never received that £30, and during the present famine I have not even attempted to collect any taxes. But, you know, our peasants are awfully lazy — the beggars won't work. There ought to be someone appointed to see that they do their work, and to flog them if they do not. Nature has given the Russian peasant a back to be flogged, and it is only by carrying out Nature's intentions that any good can be got out of him."

I soon saw that the Ispravnik was as little anxious to accompany me on my tour as I was to be honoured with his society. I finally managed to get away from him, and started off by myself to visit a few Zemski Natchalniki, to whom I had letters of introduction.

The Kazan peasants live much more comfortably than those of Central Russia. They have cups and saucers, and various other implements of civilisation, and they generally have beds. At present they are in a state of terrible destitution, and their faces are haggard with hunger. In some of the villages the Zemski Natchalnik, who accommpanied me, was implored to grant permission to use the corn which he had ordered to be stored for the spring. He was an energetic man of much courage, who had founded free bakeries, and was helping the peasants largely from his own private means. But he was far-seeing, and, in view of the probability of a complete stoppage of communications in the spring, he had ordered the peasants to put aside a portion of their allowances from the Zemstvo for this eventuality. What was surprising was that they had obeyed him. The Tartar villages were much more destitute and wretched. Many of the Tartars live in holes in the ground, covered over. They are little better than savages, and the absolute wretchedness of their condition is heartrending. They also receive relief from the Zemstvo. After I had gone the round of the huts of one of the villages the Tartars collected in a circle round me, and an aged Tartar, who spoke Russian, delivered an oration, in which he asked me to represent to the Government that it was impossible to live on bread alone, and that potatoes would be most acceptable.

The Tartar peasant women look extremely picturesque in their green and red costumes and shawls. They do not wear veils; but on meeting a man they demurely cover their faces with their hands. I am told that polygamy scarcely exists amongst the Tartars now. But then divorce is easy.

Most Tartars marry twice. Once in early life, the second time at about thirty. The first wife is divorced, and generally marries again a husband younger than herself. The men who marry a second time invariably take for their second wives very young women. This system seems to work very well.

In the districts I visited typhoid fever was raging, and I consequently became very nervous when I was one day seized with unmistakable feverish symptoms. Fortunately, the district doctor was staying over at my friend's house, and his very drastic remedies speedily set me right.

When I returned to Kazan I called on several friends and collected a few facts, which will help to convey an idea of the general state of the country. In a village, with a population of 343, there are 24 horses and 5 cows. In another village in which there used to be 1000 head of sheep there are now only 25.

The Baroness Uxkuell, writing to a friend from a village in the north, stated that she could get no bread for her own consumption. At one of the bazaars a peasant exposed his children for sale, being unable to feed them.

The peasants are committing wholesale robberies in order to get sent to Siberia, where they will at least be fed. In some villages the harvest was so bad that it was not worth collecting. The cattle were turned on the fields and allowed to eat the crops. Everywhere one meets despondency and pessimism; no one seems to have any hope.

CHAPTER XVII.

CONCLUSION.

I HAVE now travelled over most of the famine-stricken provinces, and I have been struck by the sameness of the picture. Everywhere reckless extravagance meets the eye, the forests have been cut down wantonly, the rivers are neglected, the climate is ruined; the peasant, who pays on the average taxes to the tune of £4 per head, is simply regarded as a revenue-producing unit. His welfare, his future, his mind and body, are matters of supreme indifference.

I am preparing to leave Russia much saddened by my visit. The country seems face to face with bankruptcy. The land is exhausted; the climate is changed; the existing agricultural system is a hopeless failure. The peasant and the gentleman do not understand each other; they are as widely separated as if they belonged to different nations. Instead of profiting by his emancipation the peasant has grown poorer. In many districts he has reached starvation point. The present distress has brought matters to a head, and it is everywhere acknowledged that something must be done. But what? That is the question.

There is no doubt that the Nihilists have been eagerly taking advantage of the discontent caused by the famine to extend their propaganda. Practical reformers, on the other hand, are divided in their opinions. Some still repose high hopes in the paternal guardianship of the Zemski Natchalniki. A good many hold that in Mr Henry George's land system lies the only remedy. Others, again, wish to abolish the *mir*, or Communal Assembly; and a few are even suggesting the introduction of a law of primogeniture for the peasants to prevent further subdivision of the land. Those who favour the doctrines of Mr Henry George declare that the nobles have more land than they can profitably till, and that the Government had enormous tracts of arable land lying absolutely waste. " Therefore," they say, " Mr George is the man for us ; let us nationalise the land, and expropriate the landlords."

But what the future will bring forth the future alone can show.

THE END.

COLSTON AND COMPANY, PRINTERS, EDINBURGH.

www.ingramcontent.com/pod-product-compliance
Lightning Source LLC
Chambersburg PA
CBHW031741230426
43669CB00007B/435